How NOT to be a Management Moron:

A Guide to the Art of Inspiring Leadership

Leo Whyte

© Copyright 2024 - All rights reserved.

The content contained within this book may not be reproduced, duplicated or transmitted without direct written permission from the author or the publisher.

Under no circumstances will any blame or legal responsibility be held against the publisher, or author, for any damages, reparation, or monetary loss due to the information contained within this book, either directly or indirectly.

Legal Notice:
This book is copyright protected. It is only for personal use. You cannot amend, distribute, sell, use, quote or paraphrase any part, or the content within this book, without the consent of the author or publisher.

Chapter 1: The Foundations of Inspirational Leadership

- Understanding the Role of Middle Management

- Professional Behavior and Foresight in Leadership

- Emotional Intelligence: The Key to Effective Management

Chapter 2: Crafting a Supportive Leadership Style

- How to Be a Motivating Leader

- Leading with Empathy and Encouragement

- Building Trust and Rapport with Your Team

Chapter 3: Mastering Change Management

- Embracing Change and Guiding Your Team Through It

- Effective Communication Strategies During Transitions

- Overcoming Resistance and Building Resilience

Chapter 4: Navigating Difficult Conversations and Conflict

- Breaking Bad News with Tact and Sensitivity

- Strategies for Resolving Workplace Conflicts

- Maintaining Composure and Objectivity

Chapter 5: Transforming Meetings from Mundane to Motivating

- Designing Productive and Engaging Meetings

- Encouraging Participation and Collaboration

- Meeting Follow-Up: Ensuring Accountability and Progress

Chapter 6: Cultivating Future Leaders: Coaching and Mentoring

- Identifying and Nurturing Rising Stars

- Effective Coaching Techniques for Development

- Mentoring for Long-Term Success and Growth

Chapter 7: Avoiding Common Management Pitfalls

- Recognizing and Overcoming Micromanagement Tendencies

- Balancing Control with Empowerment

- Remaining Open-Minded and Adaptable

Chapter 8: Conclusion: Embracing a Positive Leadership Journey

- Continual Growth and Development as a Leader

- Building a Legacy of Inspirational Leadership

- Reflection and Setting Future Leadership Goals

Introduction

Think back to the best manager you ever had. What made them stand out? Was it the way they listened, the confidence they instilled in you, or perhaps the way they guided you through challenges without ever taking the spotlight? Now, think about the worst manager you've had. The one who made your stomach lurch at the thought of another Monday morning. Chances are, you remember their inability to connect, their lack of empathy, or perhaps their penchant for micromanagement. What if I told you that the difference between these managers isn't innate ability, but learned skills? Skills you can acquire to become not just a manager, but the inspirational leader your team looks up to.

Welcome to "The Art of Effective Management: A Guide to Inspirational Leadership." Whether you're stepping into your first leadership role or you've been managing for a while and are ready to refine your approach, this book offers path forward. Leadership is not just about being in charge; it's about creating an environment where people can thrive, innovate, and contribute their best work.

Consider the story of a manager who thought fear was the best motivator. They believed that by keeping their team perpetually on edge, they would outperform expectations. The reality? Their team was more focused on their exit strategies than on achieving collective goals. They devised a clever "weather" system to gauge his mood, and displayed a card in a window of their offices to indicate to help each other avoid his wrath. (No fantasy I actually had this manager!) This isn't leadership; it's bullying and doesn't get results. Though the story might sound extreme, it's an illustrative example of how far off-course one can veer without a clear understanding of effective leadership. Few people actually ever receive training in how to lead and just because you're good at your job doesn't mean you'd be good at managing your team.

So, what does it mean to lead effectively? It's about more than just achieving results. It's about fostering an environment where your team feels valued, understood, and empowered to take ownership of their work. It's about inspiring others through your actions, creating trust through your integrity, and using emotional intelligence to navigate the nuances of human dynamics. It's realizing that your role is not just to steer the ship but to empower your crew to navigate the seas with confidence and creativity.

In this book, we'll explore what sets inspirational leaders apart. You'll discover the foundations of effective management, learn how to craft a leadership style that motivates and supports your team, and tackle the common pitfalls that every manager faces. Through engaging stories, practical advice, and actionable strategies, you'll gain insight into the tools you need to transform your management approach into one that inspires and elevates those around you.

To be clear from the start – this book isn't going to magically transform you into an inspirational leader overnight. You'll need to work at it and iterate repeatedly. Your style will also change depending on the people whom you manage – which will of course also change over time. This book will give you insights into the skills that you should be looking to work on, not provide a full guide in how to develop them all from scratch. That would be an encyclopedia Brittanica size book. Instead use this to gain understanding of what to consider day to day, what to work on and what to improve. Maybe go out and seek some courses on those you're struggling with or your team have fed back that you're not the best at.

Why focus so much on middle management? Because it's often the linchpin of any organization. Middle managers have the unique challenge of translating high-level strategy into actionable plans, all while managing the needs and expectations of their team. It's a role filled with potential, where the impact of great leadership is felt most directly. Yet, it's also a role where many managers struggle, caught between the pressures from above and the demands from below.

But don't worry, this isn't a doom-and-gloom portrayal of management. It's an opportunity—a chance to harness your potential and lead with impact. We'll delve into the core aspects of professional behavior and foresight, illustrating how consistency and strategic thinking can set you apart. We'll unlock the secrets of emotional intelligence, showing how understanding yourself and others can transform your leadership style. We'll explore supportive leadership, change management, and the art of navigating difficult conversations with grace and tact.

Ultimately, this book is about transformation. It's about shifting from being a manager, focused on tasks and outcomes, to becoming a leader, focused on people and potential. It's about the journey from managing to inspiring, from directing to empowering. And as you embark on this journey, remember that it's as much about personal growth as it is about professional development.

Throughout these pages, you'll find a guide that is as practical as it is insightful. Each chapter builds upon the last, creating a comprehensive roadmap for your leadership journey. There's no one-size-fits-all approach to leadership, and this book acknowledges that. Instead, it offers you the tools to discover your unique style, one that resonates with your strengths and aligns with your values.

So, whether you're looking to refine your skills or reinvent your approach, you'll find value within these pages. The goal is simple: to transform you into the kind of leader who not only achieves results but does so by inspiring and empowering those around you. A leader who is remembered not for their title, but for the impact they made on the people they led.

The journey begins here. Are you ready to become the leader your team deserves? Let's get started.

Chapter 1: The Foundations of Inspirational Leadership

Congratulations, you're about to dive headfirst into the world of inspirational leadership. It's a world that's both rewarding and, let's be honest, a bit daunting. Whether you're taking your first tentative steps into a managerial role or you're a seasoned leader who's had a wake-up call courtesy of some less-than-flattering feedback, understand this: you're not alone, and with a bit of guidance, you can transform your leadership style into something truly remarkable.

This journey we're embarking on together is all about understanding the core principles that set inspirational leaders apart from, well, the "management morons" out there. We're talking about the kind of leadership that not only guides teams to success but also inspires them to exceed their own expectations. It's about channeling your inner mentor, guiding rather than dictating, and ultimately fostering an environment where everyone can thrive.

I want to kill a big myth right now: You do not have to be able to do your teams' jobs to be able to lead the successfully. In fact, sometimes it is very advantageous not to be an absolute expert. Why? Well, often when people feel they are the experts they tend to micromanage and get frustrated when things aren't done their way or to their schedules. If you're not an expert but you *hire* experts then you're more inclined to trust their judgement and leave them feeling inspired and motivated. As the old saying goes: If you're the biggest expert or most intelligent person in the room – you're in the wrong room. Your role is to lead, guide and motivate them towards the larger goals you're all shooting for as a team and company. Manage the larger processes, resolve the roadblocks and keep the team up to standard and on time. Focus on the results not the tactics – you're a leader remember, not a manager!

Now, let's be real. Becoming an inspirational leader isn't something that happens overnight as I said before. It's a bit of trial and error, mixed with a lot of learning and unlearning. But the payoff? Oh, it's worth it. Your team will not only respect you but will also feel genuinely motivated to achieve their best work because they see you as more than just a boss—they see you as a leader worth following.

Throughout this chapter, we'll set the stage by delving into what makes middle management such a pivotal role. You'll gain insights into how professional behavior and foresight can lay the groundwork for your leadership journey. Moreover, we'll explore the critical role of emotional intelligence, ensuring you're not just managing tasks but also nurturing relationships.

So, buckle up. You're about to transform the way you lead, and in doing so, create a thriving environment that people are excited to be a part of. Let's get started on this adventure to becoming the kind of leader you—and your team—will admire.

- Understanding the Role of Middle Management

Middle management. It's often the unsung hero of the organizational ladder, a position teetering between the pressures from upper management and the needs of the team below. Many find themselves here, in this land of juggling priorities like a seasoned circus performer. Yet, it's precisely in this balancing act that you hold the potential to become an inspirational leader. Think of it as the sweet spot where you can make a significant impact on your team, your company, and, importantly, your own career trajectory.

Middle management can often feel like a rollercoaster ride, but let's break it down to understand why it's such a crucial role in any organization. You're the bridge that connects lofty company visions and strategic objectives to the ground troops—your team—who do the day-to-day work.

Your role is not just about ensuring that the tasks are completed on time but about translating those high-level goals into something tangible, actionable, and engaging for your team.

Consider the anecdote about the Moron Manager who managed to be both a micromanager and absent at the same time. They required sign-off on every minor decision from the font of an internal document to sending out quotes that used standardized pricing. At the same time, it could take weeks and weeks to get them to answer key (or even the most basic) questions with anything other than "I'll come back to you on this" or "It's on my list for today".

Sound extreme? It is again unfortunately something I have had the pleasure of experiencing directly.

Leaders (particularly those that have founded the business) are often worried about how they're perceived and how the work of their teams reflects on them (or the wider company) leading to a need to see and approve everything. The result? Having far too many things to approve and no time to actually listen to or support your team with the things that they need your guidance on.

Instead of being a bottleneck, your aim should be to streamline communication and empower your team to make decisions. Remember, being in middle management means that you have the distinct advantage of influencing both upwards and downwards. You're in a position to guide senior management's strategy by providing them with ground-level insights while simultaneously inspiring your team to align with those broader goals.

But how do you achieve this?

The first step is understanding the expectations and responsibilities that come with the role. You're not just a supervisor; you're a leader, mentor, and a catalyst for change. You have the power to create an environment that fosters innovation, collaboration, and growth.

This means actively listening to your team, providing them with the resources they need, and advocating for them when necessary. It also means being able to translate complex directives from above into clear, actionable plans that your team can rally around.

Professional behavior is another cornerstone of effective middle management. This isn't just about adhering to dress codes or punctuality—though those are certainly part of it. It's about setting a standard for how you conduct yourself and interact with others. It involves being consistent, reliable, and treating everyone with respect, whether they're a direct report or a senior executive.

Professional behavior builds trust, and trust is a fundamental building block of any successful team. The thing is, your team looks to you as a barometer for acceptable behavior. If you lose your cool under pressure, they'll think it's okay for them to do the same. If you focus on personal wellness, they'll feel it is ok to do the same when it is needed. On the flip side, if you handle challenges with grace and poise, they'll likely follow suit. If you show how to work smart and always keep your promises, they will see you practicing what you preach and do the same.

Foresight in leadership is yet another critical element. You're not expected to have a crystal ball, but you should be able to anticipate potential challenges and opportunities.

This means staying informed about industry trends, understanding your team's dynamics, and being proactive in addressing potential issues before they become problems. It's about having a strategic mindset, one that allows you to navigate the complexities of your role with a long-term view. Consider foresight as your leadership GPS, helping you chart a course through the ever-changing landscape of the corporate world.

What does having foresight actually mean though? In reality, it means thinking about the potential consequences of your words and actions, both positive and negative, ahead of saying/doing them.

As one of the best leaders I ever worked with said to me: You need to respond not react. In essence you need to take the time to think of how things will be perceived and whether it aligns with the outcome you're trying to achieve.

But let's not sugarcoat it—being in middle management isn't always glamorous. There will be days when it feels like you're caught in the crossfire, juggling conflicting demands from every direction. It's easy to become bogged down in the minutiae and lose sight of the bigger picture. However, it's crucial to remember why you decided to take on this role in the first place. Whether it's the challenge, the opportunity to make a difference, or the potential for personal and professional growth, keeping your why at the forefront will help you stay motivated and focused.

When I landed my first management position, I was lucky enough to be supported by an inspirational leader who trusted and empowered her team. By guiding rather than directing, she created an environment where team members were not just completing tasks but were actively engaged in the process. She demonstrated that leadership is not about having all the answers but about enabling others to find their own.

Did I fall on my face? Several times! Did she scold, judge or make me feel bad about it? Absolutely not. She asked two simple questions: How can I help you fix this? and What are *we* going to do differently next time?

It sounds basic but these two questions reassured me I wasn't on my own. That she supported my attempt to improve or do something new and shared the responsibility for its failure. Not only that but that she was there for me in getting things back on track. I was left feeling positive despite failure and confident that no matter what the problem was I could safely seek her guidance.

To wrap this up, the role of a middle manager is both challenging and rewarding. You have the opportunity to shape the future of your team and your organization, all while developing your own leadership skills. So, the next time you feel overwhelmed by competing demands, take a step back and remember that you're not just managing people and tasks—you're leading a team towards success.

In the coming sections, we'll explore how emotional intelligence plays a vital role in your journey as a leader, how to craft a leadership style that motivates and inspires, and how to tackle some of the common pitfalls that can trip up even the most seasoned managers. But for now, take a moment to appreciate the unique position you're in. You're not just a middle manager—you're the linchpin that holds it all together. And with the right mindset and approach, there's no limit to what you and your team can achieve.

- Professional Behavior and Foresight in Leadership

Let's dive into the heart of professional behavior and foresight in leadership. You might wonder why these concepts are emphasized so much in the context of middle management. Here's the thing: leading effectively isn't just about managing tasks or hitting targets. It's about setting an example, anticipating the needs of your team and organization, and navigating the complexities of human emotions and organizational dynamics with finesse.

Imagine walking into a meeting where everyone is on edge because no one knows what to expect from you—the manager. Will you be supportive, or will there be a storm brewing? Your demeanor, how you handle stress, and how consistently you behave set the tone for your entire team. They draw cues from you like a ship draws from its captain to navigate through choppy waters. The story of the "weather card" office should come to mind here—where the atmosphere depended so heavily on the manager's mood that team members devised a signal system to gauge whether it was safe to seek guidance. This isn't the kind of legacy you want to leave.

Professional behavior is not just about outward appearances; it's deeply rooted in how you interact, communicate, and lead. Consistency is key. People need to know that they can rely on you to be fair, to listen, and to provide guidance without bias or emotional volatility. This doesn't mean you must suppress all emotions or become a robotic presence in the office. It's about maintaining emotional balance and responding to situations in a calm, measured way, especially when things go sideways.

So, how do you cultivate this professional demeanor? Start by practicing active listening. This means truly hearing what your team is saying, beyond just the words. It's about understanding their concerns, motivations, and the underlying emotions. When your team sees that you genuinely care about their input and value their contributions, it builds trust and fosters a positive work environment. Your role then becomes less about dictating tasks and more about facilitating success.

Now let's talk about foresight. Why is it so vital? Because it allows you to steer your team in a direction that aligns with the bigger picture. It's about having the vision to see how your team's efforts contribute to broader organizational goals. This isn't just about looking at quarterly reports or year-end results. It's about understanding trends, both within your organization and in the industry at large. It's about anticipating challenges and preparing for them, so you're not constantly in crisis mode.

To develop foresight, you need to be curious. Stay informed about industry developments, new technologies, and emerging best practices. Engage with thought leaders, read extensively, and participate in professional networks. Having a broad understanding of the landscape allows you to make informed decisions and provides you with the tools to anticipate what's next. This knowledge, coupled with insights from your team, can help you prepare for future challenges and seize upcoming opportunities.

I was lucky enough that when I secured my first management position to report to an inspirational leader who guided rather than dictated. She embodied foresight by trusting her teams' insights and blending them with her strategic vision. This enabled us to not only meet expectations but often exceed them. Her leadership wasn't about having a rigid control of every detail; it was about knowing when to step back and allow the collective expertise of the team to shine through.

Foresight in leadership also means being adaptable. The business world is nothing if not unpredictable. Being able to pivot, when necessary, while still keeping your team aligned with overall goals, is a skill worth developing. It's about balancing long-term planning with short-term flexibility. This adaptability ensures your team can respond to changes swiftly without losing momentum or morale.

Let's not forget communication—a critical aspect of foresight and professional behavior. Communication is not just about disseminating information; it's about engaging with your team and creating an open dialogue. Be transparent about your expectations, the challenges you foresee, and how you plan to address them. This not only fosters trust but also empowers your team to contribute their ideas and solutions. After all, they are on the front lines and often have valuable insights into what's working and what isn't.

Another thing to bear in mind is that professional behavior and foresight are not static skills—they require continuous development and refinement. As you gain more experience, you'll find that your understanding of these concepts will deepen, and your ability to apply them will become more intuitive. Regular reflection on your leadership practice is essential. Take time to assess your interactions, your decision-making processes, and the outcomes they produce. Seek feedback from peers and mentors, and be open to making adjustments where necessary.

Lastly, remember that your journey towards becoming an inspirational leader is ongoing. There will be setbacks and challenges, but each offers an opportunity to learn and grow. By committing to professionalism and foresight, you're not just improving your leadership skills; you're creating a positive, resilient team that's ready to face whatever comes their way. As we move forward, we'll delve deeper into the crucial skill of emotional intelligence, which dovetails beautifully with what we've discussed here, and further enhances your ability to lead with impact.

- Emotional Intelligence: The Key to Effective Management

As we transition into discussing emotional intelligence, picture the office dynamics you've experienced throughout your career. Think about the managers who seemed to have an innate ability to connect with their team on a deeper level, understand their needs, and foster a supportive environment. Chances are, these individuals possessed a high degree of emotional intelligence—a trait that sets truly inspirational leaders apart from the rest.

Emotional intelligence is often described as the ability to recognize, understand, and manage our own emotions while also being able to recognize, understand, and influence the emotions of those around us. This isn't some mystical soft skill that's nice to have; it's a crucial component of effective leadership, especially in middle management where you are constantly interacting with a diverse range of personalities and emotions.

Why is emotional intelligence so important? Because it enables you to create a work environment that encourages trust, collaboration, and open communication. When team members feel heard and understood, they're more likely to engage, contribute, and go above and beyond in their roles. Remember the anecdote of the inspirational leader who used gentle questioning to lead me to optimal solutions? She wasn't dictating; she was guiding with empathy and understanding, which made all the difference.

So, let's unpack emotional intelligence and see how it can transform your approach to leadership. The first step is self-awareness. This means being conscious of your emotions and how they impact your thoughts and actions. It's about understanding your strengths and weaknesses and how they affect your leadership style.

Self-awareness allows you to approach situations objectively and respond rather than react. It helps you to remain calm under pressure, make informed decisions, and set a positive example for your team.

It's a tough skill to master though. You have to be open to critiquing yourself. You need to be aware of your flaws and how your leadership style affects others. Some soul searching is needed here and personally I find it best to work with a therapist or mentor to get some input to start with and then continue your journey of awareness from there.

Noone's perfect though and mistakes are always made. We are human after all. Self-awareness is also how you respond to this kind of thing, whether it's your mistake or a member of your team. Be aware of the way in which you react to failure. Are you defensive? Do you naturally get angry or low in mood? If so, then knowing that allows you to adjust your response accordingly.

Self-regulation is the next piece of the puzzle and naturally follows from self-awareness. It's the ability to control your impulses and manage your emotions in healthy ways. This doesn't mean suppressing your feelings or becoming emotionless; it's about acknowledging your emotions and dealing with them constructively. By practicing self-regulation, you can maintain composure in stressful situations, avoid knee-jerk reactions, and approach challenges with a clear, focused mindset. Remember, take a breath and respond rather than react.

Empathy, a cornerstone of emotional intelligence, involves understanding the emotions of others and responding with compassion. This doesn't mean being a pushover or letting emotions dictate every decision but rather being able to understand and appreciate different perspectives. Empathetic leaders are attuned to their team's emotional climate, which allows them to address concerns, provide support, and build stronger relationships. It's about being the kind of manager who knows when to push for results and when to lend a listening ear.

Social skills are another aspect of emotional intelligence that can enhance your leadership capabilities. This involves being able to communicate effectively, resolve conflicts, and foster an atmosphere of collaboration. It means being approachable, building networks, and leveraging relationships to drive team performance. Leaders with strong social skills are adept at managing relationships and navigating social complexities, which is invaluable in a middle management role.

Not everyone is an extrovert or comfortable with social situations though, and I'm not asking you to change yourself. Building up some resilience to the discomfort will help though. Small steps. Try and work out a way to bring the social elements in a way that you're comfortable with. For example, I used to bring my team together for lunches regularly. Lunches allow you to limit the time (dinners tend to hit on an expectation of drinks afterwards) and position yourself in such a way that you can talk with everyone without having to do the awkward mingle thing.

Lastly, let's talk about motivation—the drive to achieve goals and inspire others to do the same. Leaders with high emotional intelligence often have a strong internal drive for achievement and a passion for their work. They inspire their teams through their enthusiasm and commitment, which is contagious. This intrinsic motivation propels them forward, even in the face of setbacks and challenges.

The biggest motivator for a team is recognition in my experience. Celebrate the job done well, however small. Bigger successes don't hesitate to celebrate more publicly. Making sure your team see you appreciate their work but also allowing them to be seen by their peers is important.

Sometimes though, you do need to do a little pep talk to get at team back on track after a tough time.

There's no secret recipe for a pep talk. Personally, I tend to find focusing on the wider impact of the role they do helps. Are they building software that helps the agricultural industry? Then they are helping to solve world hunger. Does their work make the overall company more efficient? Then they are working to improve your day-to-day work life or maybe even get everyone a pay rise! Be creative! I've even turned it into a little whiteboard exercise where you get the team to describe who their customers are (internal and external), what the work they do is and then think about the benefit to their customers. You can then step it out to the wider industry and even community/world.

Incorporating emotional intelligence into your leadership practice isn't about ticking boxes or following a formula. It's about genuinely connecting with your team and creating a culture of trust, openness, and respect. It's about recognizing that every individual brings unique experiences and emotions to the table and valuing those differences as strengths.

To cultivate emotional intelligence, start by seeking feedback from your team and peers. Understand how your actions are perceived and where there's room for improvement. Engage in regular self-reflection to assess your emotional responses and how they impact your leadership. Consider professional development opportunities that focus on building emotional intelligence skills, such as workshops, coaching, or mentorship programs.

As we wrap up, it's clear that the foundation of inspirational leadership is built on understanding the intricate balance between professional behavior, foresight, and emotional intelligence. Each aspect complements the other, creating a holistic approach to leadership that's both effective and inspiring. The beauty of this journey is that it's ever-evolving. There's always more to learn, more to improve, and more to achieve.

By embracing these principles, you're not just enhancing your leadership skills; you're paving the way for a more engaged, motivated, and successful team. As we move forward, we'll explore how to translate these foundational skills into a supportive leadership style that motivates and encourages your team to reach new heights. Get ready to unlock the potential of your leadership journey, one thoughtfully considered step at a time.

Chapter 2: Crafting a Supportive Leadership Style

As we turn the page from laying the groundwork of inspirational leadership, it's time to dive into crafting a supportive leadership style. You've already started building the foundation with professional behavior, foresight, and emotional intelligence, and now it's about transforming those insights into tangible actions that empower and elevate your team.

Imagine a work environment where creativity flourishes, trust is inherent, and every team member feels valued and motivated. This isn't a distant dream or a utopian fantasy—it's the essence of a supportive leadership style. It's about creating a culture where your team feels safe to express ideas, take risks, and grow both professionally and personally. This chapter is all about making that vision a reality.

Moving from the basics to application, the focus now shifts to how you, as a leader, can foster an atmosphere of motivation and encouragement. This isn't about blanket positivity or ignoring challenges, but about leveraging your insights into human behavior to guide your team toward success. Supportive leadership is about being a guide rather than a dictator, a coach rather than a commander.

We'll explore what it means to be a motivating leader, one who inspires action and commitment through empathy and encouragement. It's about understanding that each team member is motivated differently and learning how to tap into those unique drivers. Whether it's through recognition, development opportunities, or simply being a source of support and stability, effective leaders know how to connect with their team on an individual level.

In crafting this leadership style, we'll delve into building trust and rapport with your team. Trust is the glue that holds a team together, and it's critical for collaboration and communication. A supportive leader knows the importance of being authentic and transparent, creating an environment where team members feel comfortable sharing their thoughts and ideas without fear of judgment or reprisal.

This chapter is also about leading with empathy—understanding your team's challenges, validating their experiences, and demonstrating that you're invested in their well-being. By fostering a culture of empathy and encouragement, you not only build stronger relationships but also enhance team morale and productivity.

As we embark on this exploration of supportive leadership, consider the leaders who have inspired you throughout your career. What qualities did they possess? How did they make you feel valued and motivated? These reflections will serve as a guide as you continue to develop your own leadership style, one that resonates with your team and drives meaningful impact.

With these goals in mind, let's explore how to transform your leadership approach to not only meet the challenges of middle management but to exceed them, creating a legacy of inspiration and growth. It's time to shape your leadership journey into one that is not only effective but also deeply rewarding for you and those you lead.

- How to Be a Motivating Leader

Stepping into the realm of supportive leadership, the first thing to grasp is the art of motivation. It's more than just rallying the troops with a pep talk or dishing out compliments; it's about understanding what makes each team member tick and helping them unlock their full potential. It's about sparking that inner drive that compels them to not just meet expectations, but to exceed them with enthusiasm and innovation.

Think of motivation as the fuel that powers your team's engine. But not all engines run on the same type of fuel. Your job as a leader is to figure out what energizes each individual. Some might thrive on recognition, while others are driven by challenges or opportunities for personal growth. A one-size-fits-all approach simply won't cut it. The Moron Manager, with his fear-driven tactics, is a quintessential example of how not to motivate. His team wasn't inspired—they were desperate to jump ship.

So, how do you become a motivating leader? Start by developing a keen understanding of your team's diverse personalities and preferences. Engage with them on a personal level. Ask questions. Listen. Show genuine interest in their aspirations and challenges. This isn't about prying into their personal lives but about demonstrating that you value them as individuals and contributors to the team. When people feel seen and appreciated, their motivation levels naturally rise.

Another key component is setting clear and attainable goals. People need to know what they're working towards and how their efforts contribute to the bigger picture. This means communicating expectations clearly and ensuring that each team member understands their role within the team. When everyone is aligned with the team's objectives, motivation follows as they see their impact on the organization's success.

Recognition is a powerful motivator that's often underutilized. It doesn't always have to be a formal award or a grand gesture. Sometimes, a simple "thank you" or a note acknowledging a job well done can make all the difference. Celebrate successes, big and small, and let your team know that their hard work is appreciated. This not only boosts individual morale but also reinforces a culture of appreciation and positivity within the team.

Providing opportunities for growth is another crucial element of motivation. This could be in the form of professional development, challenging projects, or even lateral moves within the organization that allow team members to broaden their skill sets. When people feel like they're growing and advancing in their careers, their motivation to contribute and excel increases significantly.

Don't underestimate the power of autonomy and empowerment in motivating your team.

People tend to be more motivated when they have a sense of ownership over their work. This means trusting them to make decisions and providing them with the resources and support they need to succeed. It also means stepping back and allowing them the space to innovate and find their own solutions. Remember the inspirational leader who allowed me to learn from my mistakes? Her trust in my abilities motivated me to strive for excellence.

A motivating leader also knows how to adapt their style to fit the situation and the individual. This requires flexibility and emotional intelligence—a willingness to adjust your approach based on the needs of your team and the unique circumstances you're facing. It's about balancing support with challenge, knowing when to step in and guide and when to let go and trust.

Lastly, fostering a sense of belonging and team spirit can significantly enhance motivation. When people feel like they're part of something greater than themselves, they're more likely to be engaged and committed. Encourage collaboration, celebrate team achievements, and build a culture where everyone feels included and valued.

Motivating your team is an ongoing process. It requires consistent effort and a genuine commitment to helping each person achieve their best. But the rewards are immense—a motivated team is a productive, innovative, and resilient team, ready to tackle any challenge that comes their way.

As we continue exploring supportive leadership, we'll dive deeper into leading with empathy and encouragement. These elements are closely intertwined with motivation, creating a leadership style that not only achieves results but also fosters a thriving, engaged, and satisfied team. With a clear understanding of motivation, you're well on your way to crafting a leadership style that truly inspires.

- Leading with Empathy and Encouragement

As we delve further into the essence of supportive leadership, let's cast the spotlight on leading with empathy and encouragement. These traits aren't just nice-to-haves; they're essential tools in your leadership arsenal, transforming the working environment into a place where individuals feel valued, understood, and inspired to give their best.

Empathy is about more than just putting yourself in someone else's shoes. It's about truly understanding their perspectives, emotions, and needs. In a world where work can often feel transactional, leading with empathy turns interactions into meaningful connections. When your team feels that you genuinely understand and care about their well-being, it fosters a sense of belonging and trust that's invaluable.

Consider the case of the inspirational leader who guided rather than dictated. Her empathetic approach did wonders for morale and productivity. She took the time to listen and responded thoughtfully, creating an atmosphere where people felt safe to express themselves and their ideas. This foundation of trust meant that even when challenges arose, her team felt supported and motivated to tackle them head-on.

To lead with empathy, start by actively listening. This might sound simple, but it requires you to be fully present in your conversations, setting aside distractions and preconceived notions. Listen not just to respond, but to understand. Ask open-ended questions that encourage dialogue and show genuine interest in what your team members have to say. This approach not only helps you grasp their needs and concerns but also demonstrates that you value their input.

It's also important to cultivate emotional intelligence in your leadership practice. This means being aware of your own emotions and how they impact your interactions, as well as being attuned to the emotions of those around you. By recognizing and validating the feelings of your team members, you create a supportive environment where they feel seen and heard. This doesn't mean you need to solve every problem or agree with every perspective, but it does mean acknowledging and respecting their experiences.

Encouragement, the other half of this dynamic duo, is the fuel that drives your team forward. It's about building confidence, offering support, and recognizing potential even when it's not fully realized. Encouragement is not just about praise; it's about providing constructive feedback that helps individuals grow and develop. It's about cheering them on when they succeed and offering a helping hand when they stumble.

A culture of encouragement is built through regular, honest communication. Provide feedback that is specific, actionable, and balanced. Highlight strengths and achievements while also offering guidance on areas for improvement. This approach helps your team members understand that you're invested in their development and success, which in turn boosts their confidence and motivation.

Promoting a growth mindset within your team can also enhance encouragement. Encourage them to view challenges as opportunities for learning and development rather than setbacks. Celebrate efforts and progress, not just outcomes, to reinforce the value of perseverance and resilience. This mindset shift can transform the way your team approaches their work, fostering a culture of continuous improvement and innovation.

Remember, encouragement isn't a one-size-fits-all strategy. Different individuals are motivated by different forms of recognition and support. Take the time to understand what resonates with each team member and tailor your approach accordingly. For some, it might be public recognition during team meetings, while others may appreciate a quiet word of encouragement or a handwritten note acknowledging their efforts. The key thing here is *say thank you*. You know yourself just having your boss thank you for your efforts can make a massive difference to your mindset. Noone hangs around when they don't feel appreciated.

Incorporating empathy and encouragement into your leadership style can also help you navigate difficult situations with grace. Whether it's delivering tough feedback or managing conflict, approaching these scenarios with empathy and a supportive attitude can defuse tension and lead to more productive outcomes. It shows your team that even in challenging times, you're committed to supporting them and finding solutions together.

As we continue to build on the principles of supportive leadership, it's clear that empathy and encouragement are not just soft skills—they're powerful strategies that can elevate your team's performance and satisfaction. By leading with empathy, you create a culture where individuals feel respected and valued. By fostering encouragement, you inspire your team to reach new heights and realize their full potential.

In the next section, we'll explore how to build trust and rapport with your team, further enhancing your ability to lead effectively and create a cohesive, motivated, and high-performing team. With empathy and encouragement in your toolkit, you're on the path to becoming a truly inspirational leader.

- Building Trust and Rapport with Your Team

As we round out our exploration of supportive leadership, it's time to delve into the linchpin of any successful team: trust and rapport. These elements are the bedrock upon which all other leadership qualities are built. Without them, even the most well-intentioned efforts at motivation or empathy can fall flat. In essence, trust and rapport create the fertile ground where the seeds of motivation, empathy, and encouragement can grow.

Imagine a team where trust is shaky—a place where people second-guess each other, hold back ideas, and approach every interaction with a hint of skepticism. Noone is willing to take a shot at something new for fear of blame if it doesn't work. It's hardly the environment for creativity or productivity to flourish. Now picture a team where trust and rapport are strong. Here, team members feel free to express ideas, admit mistakes, and collaborate wholeheartedly. This is the kind of environment you want to cultivate.

Building trust starts with consistency. Your team needs to see that your actions align with your words. If you say you're going to do something, follow through. If you promise to support their development, make sure you're providing the necessary resources and opportunities. Consistency demonstrates reliability, and reliability fosters trust.

Transparency is another cornerstone of trust. Be open about decisions, changes, and challenges. Share the rationale behind your choices and invite your team to contribute their thoughts and ideas. This openness not only builds trust but also empowers your team to feel involved and valued. When people understand the bigger picture and their role within it, they're more likely to be invested and engaged.

Rapport is about building genuine connections with your team. It's about showing interest in their lives beyond work and understanding them as individuals with unique experiences and aspirations. This doesn't mean crossing professional boundaries, but rather acknowledging the human element in every interaction. Take time to engage in informal conversations, celebrate milestones, and show empathy in times of difficulty.

Consider my story of my first manager, who trusted her team and guided us with gentle questions. She didn't just build trust through her actions but also fostered rapport by showing genuine interest in the well-being and development of her team. She knew when to push and when to lend support, creating a balanced dynamic that encouraged growth.

Feedback is a powerful tool for building trust and rapport. When delivered constructively, it shows your team that you're committed to their success. Create a feedback-rich environment where open communication is encouraged, and feedback flows both ways. Be receptive to feedback from your team and demonstrate that you value their perspectives. This two-way street of communication strengthens trust and fosters mutual respect. Don't wait for the annual review. Steer your ship with little nudges as they are needed not huge lurching turns once or twice a year.

My biggest tip with feedback is: don't try and sugar coat it. Everyone is aware of the feedback sandwich (negative comment surrounded on either side with positive) these days so it tends not to work the way you expect. Instead, be open and transparent. "Overall, your performance this year has been exceptional but there's a couple of things I'd like you to work on." or "There's a lot we need to work on here and I'd like to work through my feedback and how *we* are going to work together to get things back on track."

Part of building trust and rapport involves being authentic. Authenticity means being true to your values and leading with integrity. It's about admitting mistakes and owning up to shortcomings. When your team sees that you're genuine and honest, they're more likely to trust and respect you. Authentic leaders inspire loyalty and commitment because they're relatable and trustworthy.

Trust and rapport are not built overnight; they require ongoing effort and nurturing. Regularly assess the health of your team dynamics and be proactive in addressing any trust issues that arise. Encourage team-building activities and opportunities for collaboration, as these can strengthen relationships and enhance trust. Yeah, I know, no one likes enforced fun. Once you get over the initial hurdle of that feeling they do actually work. The key is choosing the right activity for the team. If the team are very outdoorsy then maybe a professional treasure hunt? If they're more academic maybe an escape room?

As you weave trust and rapport into the fabric of your leadership style, remember that you're not just building a team; you're creating a community. A community where people feel safe to be their authentic selves, where they're encouraged to take risks and innovate, and where they're supported in their growth and development.

Another big tip here: *do not* whatever you do start talking about "we are a family here". No, no you're not. You don't choose your family (let's put chosen family to the side, that's something very different.) Families fight. They fall out with each other. Sometimes families hate each other and cut off all communication. Is that what you're saying your business is? That's how some people will interpret it. You're not a family, you're a team. Teams work together. Teams support each other. Most importantly, if the team isn't working out for someone...they can leave!

As we wrap up this chapter on supportive leadership, it's clear that motivation, empathy, encouragement, trust, and rapport are all interconnected. Together, they form a cohesive strategy for leading a team that's not only high-performing but also engaged and satisfied. These elements are more than just strategies—they're a commitment to leading with heart and intention.

With this foundation in place, you're equipped to guide your team through challenges, celebrate successes, and build a work environment that people are proud to be a part of. As we move into the next chapter, we'll explore how to master change management, helping your team navigate transitions with resilience and confidence. So, take a moment to reflect on the supportive leadership principles we've covered, and get ready to lead your team into new territories of growth and success.

Chapter 3: Mastering Change Management

As we venture into the crucial terrain of change management, take a moment to consider your own experiences with change in the workplace. Chances are, you've witnessed transitions that went smoothly and others that felt like attempting to steer a ship through stormy seas without a compass. Change is a constant in the business world, yet it remains one of the most challenging aspects for any team to navigate. But here's the good news: with the right approach, you can guide your team through change with confidence and resilience.

Change management is about more than just implementing new processes or technology. It's about managing the emotional and psychological impacts that come with any shift in the status quo. As a leader, your role is to be the steady hand that keeps everyone grounded while navigating the uncharted waters of transformation. This chapter is dedicated to equipping you with the tools and insights needed to master this delicate balance.

Picture the Moron Manager, who, in an attempt to introduce new procedures, merely sent out a mass email dictating the changes without any prior discussion or support. The result? Confusion, resistance, and a team left feeling undervalued and disenfranchised. Contrast this with the inspirational leader who took the time to engage her team to engage in the change process, listening to them, communicating ahead of the change, addressing their concerns and involving them in creating solutions *before* the change is implemented. She understood that successful change relies heavily on buy-in and collaboration, and she leveraged these to turn potential resistance into enthusiasm.

One of the first steps to effective change management is communication. It might sound like a cliche, but it's true—communication is key. Your team needs to understand the why behind the change. Why is it happening now? What are the benefits? How will it impact their day-to-day work? By answering these questions upfront, you set the stage for transparency and reduce the fear of the unknown.

In this chapter, we'll explore strategies for communicating effectively during change, ensuring that your team feels informed, involved, and valued. We'll discuss the importance of listening to feedback, adapting your approach based on team insights, and being open to new ideas that can enhance the change process.

Another critical element of change management is recognizing and addressing resistance. Change is inherently uncomfortable, and it's natural for people to resist leaving their comfort zones. Understanding the root causes of resistance—whether it's fear of the unknown, perceived loss of control, or simply a preference for the familiar—allows you to address these concerns empathetically and strategically.

This chapter will also guide you in building resilience within your team. Change can be unsettling, but with the right support, your team can emerge stronger and more adaptable. We'll look at how to foster a growth mindset, encourage flexibility, and provide the resources necessary to navigate transitions successfully.

As you embark on mastering change management, remember that your role isn't just about implementing new systems or processes; it's about guiding people through transformation. It's about balancing stability with innovation, and steadfast leadership with open-mindedness. By leading with empathy and clarity, you can turn change into an opportunity for growth, innovation, and improved team dynamics.

So, get ready to delve into the nuances of change management, arming yourself with the insights and strategies needed to lead your team through transitions with grace and confidence. This journey will not only enhance your leadership skills but also strengthen your team's ability to thrive in the face of change, setting the stage for continued success in an ever-evolving landscape.

- Embracing Change and Guiding Your Team Through It

Navigating change can feel a bit like trying to hit a moving target. Just when you think you've got a handle on things, something shifts and suddenly everything's up in the air again. Yet, for those who master it, change management becomes less of a daunting task and more of an exciting challenge. The secret lies in embracing change as an opportunity rather than an obstacle.

Consider again the chaos sown by the Moron Manager who dropped changes like bombshells without a moment's thought to how his team would react. It wasn't just the lack of communication; it was the complete disregard for how these changes would impact everyday work life. His team was left scrambling, confused, and frustrated, turning what could have been a smooth transition into a morale-draining mess. He acted like a dictator and gave the hidden message, "I know better than you, you're just employees, I don't care about your opinions or work environment."

Contrast this with the inspired leader who approached change with a different mindset. She understood that change, at its core, is about people. It's about understanding their needs, addressing their concerns, and involving them in the process. Her approach wasn't to impose change, but to guide her team through it, transforming potential resistance into proactive engagement.

To embrace change effectively, you must first cultivate a mindset of openness and curiosity. This means seeing change as an opportunity to learn, innovate, and improve. It's about asking yourself and your team, "What can we gain from this change?" rather than dwelling on what might be lost. This shift in perspective can make all the difference in how change is perceived and embraced by your team.

One of the most effective ways to guide your team through change is by creating a compelling vision. A vision provides direction and purpose, helping people to see beyond the immediate discomfort to the potential benefits that lie ahead. It paints a picture of what success looks like and inspires people to work towards it. When your team understands the bigger picture and their role within it, they're more likely to be motivated and willing to invest in the change.

Creating this vision requires clear, consistent communication. Share the rationale behind the change and the positive outcomes you anticipate. Be transparent about any challenges and how you plan to address them. Encourage questions and discussions and be prepared to provide honest answers. This openness not only builds trust but also empowers your team to feel involved and invested.

Involve your team in the change process as much as possible. Encourage them to share their ideas and insights and let them contribute to shaping the path forward. After all, they're the ones who will be implementing and living with the change on a daily basis. By tapping into their expertise and perspectives, you not only improve the quality of your solutions but also increase buy-in and commitment.

Recognize that change can trigger a wide range of emotions, from excitement to anxiety. Acknowledge these feelings and provide support to help your team navigate them. Whether it's through one-on-one conversations, team meetings, or informal check-ins, show empathy and understanding. This doesn't mean you have to have all the answers or eliminate every concern, but it does mean creating a space where people feel comfortable expressing their emotions.

Another important aspect of embracing change is flexibility. Change rarely follows a straight path, and there will undoubtedly be unforeseen challenges and adjustments along the way. Being adaptable means being willing to shift strategies, rethink timelines, and reassess priorities as new information emerges. Encourage your team to adopt this flexible mindset, emphasizing that it's okay to adjust course as long as you stay aligned with the overall vision.

To build resilience in the face of change, focus on fostering a culture of continuous learning and improvement. Encourage your team to view setbacks as opportunities to learn and grow rather than as failures. Provide resources and support for skill development, ensuring that your team has the tools they need to succeed in the new environment. Celebrate progress, no matter how small, to reinforce a sense of achievement and momentum.

Remember, as a leader, your attitude towards change sets the tone for your team. Approach it with optimism, curiosity, and a willingness to learn, and your team will likely follow suit. By embracing change with a positive mindset and a clear strategy, you're not just managing transitions—you're empowering your team to thrive in an ever-changing landscape.

As we delve deeper into this chapter, we'll explore effective communication strategies during transitions and how to overcome resistance, ensuring your team remains aligned and motivated. With these skills in hand, you'll be well-equipped to transform potential obstacles into opportunities for growth and success.

- Effective Communication Strategies During Transitions

In the midst of navigating change, communication stands out as your most powerful tool. It's the lifeline that connects you to your team and ensures everyone is rowing in the same direction. But communication during change isn't just about disseminating information; it's about creating dialogue, fostering understanding, and building confidence. It's about ensuring that your team feels informed, involved, and ready to tackle the challenges ahead.

Think back to the Moron Manager's approach—an abrupt email with no context, no dialogue, and no opportunity for feedback. His team was left in the dark, struggling to make sense of the changes thrust upon them. Contrast this with the inspirational leader who took the time to communicate openly and consistently, creating an environment where her team felt prepared and supported. Her approach transformed what could have been a chaotic transition into a coordinated effort.

Effective communication during change starts with clarity. Your team needs to understand the what, why, and how of the change. What exactly is changing? Why is this change necessary? How will it impact their roles and responsibilities? Providing clear, concise answers to these questions helps alleviate uncertainty and sets the stage for a smooth transition.

But clarity alone isn't enough. Communication needs to be a two-way street. Encourage your team to ask questions, share their concerns, and provide feedback. Create channels for open dialogue, whether it's through regular team meetings, one-on-one conversations, or anonymous feedback mechanisms. This not only helps you identify potential issues early on but also demonstrates that you value your team's input and are committed to addressing their needs.

A key component of effective communication is timing. Don't wait until every detail is finalized before engaging your team. Share information as it becomes available, even if you don't have all the answers yet. This transparency builds trust and keeps your team informed, reducing the likelihood of rumors and misinformation taking hold. Be honest about what you know, what you don't know, and what steps you're taking to fill in the gaps.

Empathy is another crucial element of communication during change. Recognize that change can be unsettling and that different people will react in different ways. Some may embrace the change with enthusiasm, while others may feel anxious or resistant. Acknowledge these emotions and provide support to help your team navigate them. Show that you understand their perspectives and are there to help them succeed.

Listening is just as important as speaking. Take the time to truly listen to your team's concerns and perspectives. Validate their feelings and respond with empathy and understanding. This doesn't mean you'll be able to address every concern or grant every request, but it does mean creating an environment where people feel heard and valued. Sometimes, simply knowing that their concerns are being acknowledged can make a significant difference in how team members perceive and engage with the change.

It's also important to tailor your communication to suit your audience. Different team members may have different needs and preferences when it comes to receiving information. Some may prefer detailed written documents, while others might respond better to face-to-face conversations or visual presentations. Be flexible in your approach and be willing to adapt your communication style to ensure your message is understood and resonates with your team.

Creating a sense of inclusion is vital. Involve your team in the transition process as much as possible. Encourage them to contribute their ideas and insights, and let them play an active role in shaping the change. This involvement not only enhances the quality of your solutions but also fosters a sense of ownership and commitment, increasing the likelihood of successful implementation.

As you communicate, reinforce the vision and goals of the change. Remind your team of the bigger picture and how their efforts contribute to it. Celebrate milestones and progress to maintain momentum and morale. By keeping the vision front and center, you help your team stay focused and motivated, even when challenges arise.

Remember, communication is an ongoing process. It doesn't end once the change has been implemented. Continue to provide updates, address concerns, and celebrate successes to keep your team engaged and aligned. Be proactive in seeking feedback and be open to making adjustments based on what you learn.

As we continue our exploration of change management, we'll dive into strategies for overcoming resistance and building resilience within your team. With effective communication as your foundation, you're well on your way to leading your team through change with confidence and clarity, transforming potential obstacles into opportunities for growth and success.

- Overcoming Resistance and Building Resilience

As we bring this chapter on change management to a close, it's time to tackle one of the most persistent hurdles in any transition: resistance. Resistance to change is as old as time itself, and it can manifest in a myriad of ways—from overt pushback to quiet disengagement and quiet quitting. Yet, it's in overcoming this resistance that you can truly transform challenges into opportunities for growth and foster a resilient team ready to embrace the future.

Let's revisit the tale of the Moron Manager who bulldozed through change, leaving his team feeling unimportant and ignored. Resistance was rampant, not because the changes lacked merit, but because the approach alienated those who needed to drive the change forward. Contrast this with my inspirational leader who recognized resistance as a signal, not a roadblock. She listened, adapted, and addressed concerns head-on, turning potential opposition into support. She couldn't always change the process to suit our desires but at least we understood why and felt heard.

The first step in overcoming resistance is understanding its root causes. Resistance often stems from fear—fear of the unknown, fear of failure, or fear of losing control. It can also arise from a perceived lack of value or relevance in the proposed changes. By identifying the underlying reasons for resistance, you can tailor your approach to address these concerns directly.

Empathy plays a vital role in this process. Approach resistance with curiosity rather than defensiveness. Engage in conversations to understand the perspectives of those who are struggling with the change. Demonstrating empathy and acknowledging their feelings can help to diffuse tension and open the door to more constructive dialogue.

Involving your team in the change process is another crucial and powerful antidote to resistance. Encourage them to contribute their ideas and insights, and empower them to take ownership of the transition. When people feel involved and valued, they're more likely to invest in the change and work collaboratively towards its success.

Transparency is key. I can't say it enough. Be open about the challenges and limitations of the change, as well as the benefits. Share your thought process and the rationale behind decisions. This openness builds trust and reduces skepticism, helping to align your team with the change objectives.

Provide support and resources to help your team navigate the transition. This might include training, mentorship, or simply additional time and space to adjust. By equipping your team with the tools they need, you reduce anxiety and increase confidence in their ability to adapt and succeed.

Sometimes, despite your best efforts, resistance persists. In these cases, it's important to remain patient and persistent. Change is a journey, not a sprint, and it may take time for some individuals to fully embrace it. Continue to communicate openly, provide support, and celebrate small victories along the way to maintain momentum and morale.

Building resilience within your team is equally important. Resilience is about more than just bouncing back from setbacks; it's about growing stronger through challenges. Encourage a growth mindset, where mistakes are seen as opportunities for learning and development rather than failures. Foster a culture of continuous improvement, where experimentation and innovation are encouraged and celebrated.

Consider the story of the inspirational leader who fostered resilience by empowering us to learn from mistakes. She understood that failure was a stepping stone to success and encouraged her team to take calculated risks and learn from the outcomes. This approach not only strengthened their ability to adapt to change but also fostered a sense of confidence and capability.

As we transition to the next phase of our exploration, remember that managing change is an ongoing process. It requires patience, empathy, and a commitment to learning and growth. By embracing change with an open mind and a supportive approach, you're not just navigating transitions—you're leading your team toward a more resilient, innovative, and successful future.

In the following chapter, we'll delve into navigating difficult conversations and conflict, equipping you with the skills to handle challenging situations with tact and sensitivity. As you continue your journey toward inspirational leadership, these new skills will further enhance your ability to lead with confidence and compassion. So, as we move forward, take these insights on change management to heart, and prepare to tackle the next set of challenges with renewed energy and purpose.

Chapter 4: Navigating Difficult Conversations and Conflict

As we shift gears from managing change to a subject that can send shivers down even the most seasoned leader's spine—difficult conversations and conflict—let's acknowledge a simple truth: No one particularly enjoys conflict. Yet, navigating these uncomfortable waters is an essential part of effective leadership. Whether it's delivering bad news, addressing performance issues, or managing interpersonal disputes, handling difficult conversations with sensitivity and skill is crucial for maintaining a harmonious and productive team environment.

Think back to times when tension simmered beneath the surface, and conversations were avoided like the plague, resulting in misunderstandings and festering resentment. Or recall the Moron Manager, who tackled conflict with all the subtlety of a brick through a plate glass window, often leaving his team in a state of turmoil. Compare that to the inspirational leader who approached challenging conversations with tact and empathy, transforming potential conflict into opportunities for clarity and growth.

Handling difficult conversations isn't about having all the answers or controlling every outcome. It's about creating a safe space where issues can be addressed openly and constructively. It's about listening as much as speaking and understanding that your role is to facilitate a resolution, not to win an argument.

This chapter is dedicated to equipping you with the tools to approach these situations with confidence and composure. We'll explore strategies for breaking bad news with tact, resolving workplace conflicts with objectivity, and maintaining your cool when emotions run high. By mastering these skills, you'll not only defuse tension but also foster a culture of trust and respect within your team.

The first step in navigating difficult conversations is preparation. Going in unprepared is like walking into a storm without an umbrella. Understand the issue at hand, gather the necessary information, and have a clear idea of the outcome you're hoping to achieve. This groundwork will provide a solid foundation for a constructive conversation.

Empathy and active listening will be your greatest allies in these situations. Approach conversations with an open mind, and be prepared to listen to the other person's perspective. Acknowledge their feelings and validate their experiences, even if you don't agree with them. This doesn't mean conceding your position, but rather showing respect and understanding.

We'll also look at the importance of language and tone. The words you choose and the way you deliver them can have a significant impact on the conversation's outcome.

By communicating with clarity and respect, you set the tone for a productive dialogue and minimize the risk of defensiveness or escalation.

Throughout this chapter, we'll weave in practical examples and anecdotes to illustrate these concepts in action. By the end of it, you'll have a toolkit of strategies to handle difficult conversations with confidence and empathy, transforming them from dreaded tasks into opportunities for growth and resolution.

So, take a deep breath and get ready to delve into the art of handling difficult conversations. With the right approach, you'll not only resolve conflicts but also strengthen the bonds within your team, paving the way for a more cohesive and supportive work environment. As we explore these skills, remember that each conversation is an opportunity to lead with integrity and compassion, reinforcing your role as an inspirational leader.

- Breaking Bad News with Tact and Sensitivity

Diving headlong into the art of tackling tough conversations, let's begin with the delicate task of breaking bad news. It's never easy, and it's rarely pleasant, but delivering difficult news with grace and sensitivity is a hallmark of inspirational leadership. Whether it's performance feedback, company restructuring, or even letting someone go, how you handle this process can significantly impact not just the individual involved but the entire team's morale and cohesion.

Picture the anxiety that grips a team when bad news is delivered clumsily, sowing confusion and fear. This is often due to the lack of clear communication or the poor handling of the message itself.

A Moron Manager' tends to blurt out bad news without preparation or empathy, leaving a trail of unrest. In stark contrast, consider an inspirational leader who approached these conversations with care, ensuring that even the toughest news was delivered with respect and understanding.

To break bad news effectively, preparation is paramount. It's crucial to understand the issue inside and out, anticipate potential reactions, and have a clear message. This doesn't mean scripting every word, but ensuring you're informed and ready to address the concerns that will inevitably arise. Preparation demonstrates that you care about the impact of the news and are committed to addressing it thoughtfully.

When it's time to deliver the news, choose your setting wisely. A private, quiet space where the conversation can occur without interruptions is ideal. This shows respect for the person receiving the news and provides a safe environment for an open discussion. Avoid public places or situations where confidentiality could be compromised. I know it's common sense but you'd be surprised how many Moron Managers choose the company canteen to break bad news over coffee!

Personally, when the news it very delicate, and it is going to be a virtual meeting, I write myself a script to read. This ensures that your own emotions don't get the better of you, you don't start waffling and can be controlled. In person meetings are a different scenario. Turning up and reading something makes it very formal and immediately puts up barriers. Instead, practice. Keep it very concise so that you can easily convey it without getting tongue tied. At most take a couple of bullet points with you to keep.

Empathy is your ally throughout this process. Start the conversation by acknowledging the difficulty of the news and expressing your understanding of how it might impact the individual. This doesn't mean sugarcoating the issue or avoiding the truth, but rather showing that you're considerate of their feelings and are there to support them through the process.

As you deliver the news, be direct yet compassionate. Avoid jargon or euphemisms that might confuse or obscure the message. Clarity is crucial. Explain the situation, the reasons behind the decision, and any relevant context honestly. This transparency helps foster understanding, even if the news is hard to accept.

Starting the meeting is the hardest part in reality. Moron Managers dash straight into and often blindside people, causing overly emotional reactions. My recommendation with any difficult conversation is start with that transparency. I'll usually start with something like, "OK, so this is going to be a difficult/uncomfortable conversation. I'm sorry for that but it is an important one."

Then take a moment. Breathe, let them breathe and prepare themselves. Horrible to hear but it shows empathy and gives them (and you) a moment to prepare themselves.

Once the news is shared, give the individual time to process it. Everyone reacts differently—some might need to ask questions, others might need a moment of silence, and some might express immediate emotion. Others might need to come back to you later to discuss it once it has sunk in. Be prepared to handle these reactions with patience and understanding. Offer reassurance and support, and encourage an open dialogue about how best to move forward.

Next, involve the individual in discussing the next steps. Whether it's developing a plan to address performance issues, exploring opportunities elsewhere, or providing resources to aid the transition, empower them to take an active role in shaping their path forward. This involvement can help mitigate feelings of helplessness and foster a sense of control over the situation.

Where possible give them space and time to process. Let them go home or sign off for a few hours if appropriate. This serves two purposes. It shows empathy and lets them see that you understand how hard this was to hear and that they will need some time to gather themselves.

It also prevents them taking those emotions and throwing them around at everyone else. Think of the colleague who had a bad end of year review and came back to their desk swearing how unfair it was and calling their manager all the names under the sun. Did you feel motivated after hearing it? How much time did you waste listening to them? Will you go into your review with a positive attitude as a result? Given them space, let them calm down and it will minimize this impact.

It's also important to follow up after the conversation. A quick email or meeting to check in shows that you're committed to supporting them through the change. This follow-up reinforces that your support wasn't limited to the conversation itself but extends into the future, helping to maintain trust and rapport.

The ripple effects of how you break bad news extend beyond the individual directly involved. Your team will observe your approach and, consciously or not, take cues from it. Handling difficult conversations with integrity and empathy sets a precedent for the entire team, fostering a culture of respect and transparency.

In the broader scope of leadership, mastering the art of breaking bad news is about more than just delivering a difficult message. It's about maintaining dignity, fostering trust, and demonstrating that even in challenging times, you are a leader who cares about people first. It's about showing that you can navigate the toughest aspects of leadership with grace and compassion, leaving a positive impact even in the face of adversity.

As we continue to explore the nuances of handling difficult conversations, we'll next delve into strategies for resolving workplace conflicts. This essential skill will further enhance your ability to maintain harmony and productivity within your team, reinforcing your role as an empathetic and effective leader. With these tools in hand, you're well on your way to transforming potential conflicts into opportunities for growth and cohesion.

I want to give you one further tip here. If you know one of your peer managers is set to give bad news, check in on them afterwards. No one considers the impact that these activities have on the managers themselves. I've made really hard redundancies in the past and not a soul has checked in. Your colleagues will thank you for it and it will strengthen your internal relationships and respect as a result.

You never know the impact that kindness can have on someone.

- Strategies for Resolving Workplace Conflicts

Turning our attention now to resolving workplace conflicts, we enter a realm that tests even the most seasoned leaders. Conflict is an inevitable part of working closely with others. Wherever diverse personalities and viewpoints coexist, there's potential for disagreement. But conflict, when managed effectively, can be a catalyst for growth, innovation, and stronger team dynamics. The key lies in not avoiding conflict, but navigating it with skill and empathy.

Consider our Moron Manager, whose approach to conflict was either to ignore it entirely and hope it goes away or to assert dominance with little regard for resolution – going in and placing blame, rolling their eyes and belittling people.

Their team, caught in a cycle of unresolved tensions, find themselves frustrated and disengaged. Now think of our inspirational leader who viewed conflict as an opportunity. By addressing issues head-on in a constructive manner, she not only resolved disagreements but also strengthened team unity and understanding.

The first step in resolving conflict is recognizing its root cause. Often, conflict arises from miscommunication, differing expectations, or clashing interpersonal styles. By identifying the underlying issue, you can tailor your approach to address it directly, rather than just treating the symptoms. This clarity helps in crafting a resolution that is both effective and sustainable.

Approaching conflict with an open mind and a neutral stance is crucial. As a leader, your role is to facilitate dialogue, not to take sides. Set the stage for an honest conversation by creating a safe, neutral environment where those involved can express their perspectives without fear of judgment or retribution. This atmosphere of trust encourages openness and honesty, laying the groundwork for resolution.

Active listening is indispensable in these situations. Listen not just to the words being spoken, but to the emotions and motivations behind them. Acknowledge each person's feelings and validate their experiences. This doesn't mean you have to agree with every point but showing that you understand and respect their perspectives can help defuse tension and build rapport.

Once the issues and perspectives have been aired, work collaboratively to explore potential solutions. Encourage all parties to contribute ideas and be open to compromise. This collaborative approach not only fosters a sense of ownership and commitment to the resolution but also often leads to more innovative and effective solutions. Remember, the goal is not to "win" the conflict but to find a resolution that respects everyone's needs and aligns with team objectives.

Clear, open communication is essential throughout the process. Ensure that everyone involved understands the agreed-upon resolution and the steps required to implement it. This clarity helps prevent misunderstandings and ensures that all parties are on the same page moving forward.

Accountability is another crucial element of conflict resolution. Once a resolution is reached, set clear expectations and responsibilities for each party. Follow up regularly to ensure that commitments are being met and that the resolution is holding. This follow-through reinforces the importance of accountability and helps maintain the progress achieved.

In some cases, professional development or team-building activities can be beneficial in addressing underlying issues and preventing future conflicts. Workshops on communication skills, emotional intelligence, or diversity and inclusion can equip your team with the tools they need to navigate interpersonal challenges more effectively. These proactive measures can strengthen team cohesion and resilience, reducing the likelihood of conflict down the line.

Maintaining a positive team culture is also integral to minimizing conflict. Encourage a culture of respect, where diverse perspectives are valued and open communication is the norm. Celebrate team successes and foster an environment where collaboration and mutual support are prioritized. This positive atmosphere helps build strong relationships and trust, creating a more harmonious and productive work environment.

As you hone your skills in conflict resolution, remember that each situation is unique. There's no one-size-fits-all solution, and what works in one scenario may not be effective in another. Flexibility, empathy, and a commitment to finding constructive solutions are your greatest assets in navigating these complex dynamics.

Resolving workplace conflicts is more than just keeping the peace. It's about fostering a culture of understanding and collaboration, where differences are seen as strengths and challenges are met with resilience and creativity. By approaching conflict with an open mind and a focus on resolution, you'll not only strengthen your team's dynamics but also reinforce your role as a supportive and effective leader.

As we delve into the final section of this chapter, we'll explore strategies for maintaining composure and objectivity even in the most challenging conversations. With these skills, you'll be well-prepared to lead with confidence and empathy, turning potential conflicts into opportunities for growth and cohesion.

- Maintaining Composure and Objectivity

As we close our exploration of handling difficult conversations and conflict, let's focus on a crucial leadership quality: maintaining composure and objectivity. It's one thing to understand the theory of conflict resolution and communication, but it's quite another to put it into practice, especially when emotions are high and stakes are even higher. Keeping your cool not only helps defuse tension but also sets the tone for a constructive dialogue.

Picture the times when a leader lost their composure. Maybe you've seen it firsthand, a raised voice, a dismissive attitude, a roll of the eyes, a tutt, or even a sudden withdrawal.

The result? Often, it escalates the situation, undermines trust, and leaves a lasting negative impression.

On the other hand, leaders who maintain calmness and objectivity provide a stabilizing presence, allowing for clearer thinking and better solutions.

Maintaining composure starts with self-awareness. Recognizing your emotional triggers and understanding how they affect your responses is key. This awareness allows you to pause, reflect, and choose a measured response rather than reacting impulsively. It's about taking a deep breath and giving yourself the space to respond thoughtfully rather than reflexively.

Objectivity requires a commitment to understanding all sides of a conversation. It means setting aside personal biases and focusing on the facts and the issue at hand. This doesn't imply being detached or indifferent, but rather balancing empathy with impartiality. By focusing on the problem rather than personal grievances, you help guide the conversation toward resolution rather than conflict.

One strategy of my to maintain composure is to practice active listening. When you're truly focused on understanding the other person's perspective, it's easier to set aside your own emotions and remain present in the conversation. This not only aids in keeping you calm but also demonstrates respect and understanding toward the other party, which can defuse tension and foster a more open dialogue.

Active listening is hard though when you're trying not to lose it completely with the Moron Manager you're having to interact with, right? My tip is to keep a small whiteboard (if you're remote) or notebook in front of you. When questions or feelings arise quickly note them down and refocus on the person who is talking. This stops you blurting things out and ensures you don't focus on remembering your questions but instead listening. I admit writing down my initial thoughts has really helped me to respond rather than react over the years.

Another helpful approach is to frame conflicts as opportunities for growth and learning. Every disagreement or difficult conversation is a chance to better understand your team, your leadership style, and the dynamics within the group. By viewing these situations as part of the journey toward improved collaboration and team cohesion, you can approach them with a positive, constructive mindset.

Consider the inspirational leader who consistently approached conflict with a calm, composed demeanor. Her ability to remain objective and focused on solutions, even in the most challenging situations, was a testament to her leadership skills. She knew that her composure set the tone for her team, who, in turn, learned to handle their own disputes with greater maturity and understanding.

Remember, maintaining composure doesn't mean suppressing emotions or ignoring problems. It's about acknowledging them, managing them, and channeling them in a way that's conducive to resolution. This balance of emotional intelligence and strategic thinking is what sets strong leaders apart.

When you find yourself in the midst of conflict, it can be helpful to take a step back and assess the situation from a different perspective. Sometimes, a short break or a change of scenery can provide the clarity needed to approach the issue with renewed focus and objectivity. Don't hesitate to take a moment if you find your emotions starting to take the wheel.

As we prepare to transition to the next chapter, reflect on the skills and insights gained in handling difficult conversations and conflict. By mastering these areas, you're not only able to resolve issues more effectively but also to foster a culture of trust and collaboration within your team. These competencies will serve as a strong foundation as we move forward to explore new challenges and opportunities in your leadership journey.

The next phase of our journey will delve into transforming meetings from mundane to motivating. With the skills of communication and conflict resolution under your belt, you're well-equipped to enhance these gatherings, ensuring they're both productive and engaging. As we step into this new chapter, take with you the confidence and composure developed here, ready to tackle the next set of leadership challenges with clarity and purpose.

Chapter 5: Transforming Meetings from Mundane to Motivating

Stepping into the realm of meetings, it's time to transform these often-dreaded events from mundane to motivating. Meetings are a staple of professional life, yet too many of them are unproductive, leaving participants feeling like they've wasted precious time. But what if meetings could be a source of energy and inspiration instead of a drain? What if they could be the catalyst for innovation and collaboration, driving your team forward with purpose and clarity?

Consider the stereotype of long, tedious meetings where attention wanes, and enthusiasm is conspicuously absent. We've all been there, watching the clock, wondering why we're there in the first place. The Moron Manager operated like this, running meetings that were more akin to monologues, leaving attendees disengaged and disconnected from any actionable outcomes. Contrast this with the inspirational leader who turned meetings into dynamic exchanges of ideas, where each participant felt valued and heard, and left with a clear sense of direction and purpose.

The aim of this chapter is to equip you with the tools to revolutionize your approach to meetings, ensuring they're not just necessary, but impactful. We'll delve into strategies for designing meetings that are both productive and engaging, ensuring every session is an opportunity to galvanize your team and propel projects forward.

The first step in transforming meetings is understanding their purpose. Every meeting should have a clear objective and desired outcome. Is the goal to brainstorm ideas, solve a problem, update project status, or make critical decisions? By defining the purpose upfront, you set the framework for a focused and effective session.

Equally important is the preparation that goes into a meeting. Send out agendas and relevant materials ahead of time, allowing participants to come prepared and ready to contribute. This not only maximizes the value of the meeting but also demonstrates respect for everyone's time and expertise.

In this chapter, we'll explore how to encourage active participation and collaboration. It's about creating an inclusive environment where every voice is heard and diverse perspectives are valued. We'll discuss techniques for facilitating discussions, managing time effectively, and keeping the meeting on track.

Remember the inspirational leader who fostered a culture of open dialogue and active engagement? Her meetings were a testament to the power of collective input. By asking thoughtful questions and encouraging diverse viewpoints, she ensured that her team felt invested in the outcomes and inspired to act.

We'll also address the importance of meeting follow-up—an often-overlooked aspect. A meeting doesn't end when everyone leaves the room. Ensuring accountability and progress requires clear documentation of decisions made and action items assigned. We'll look at how to implement effective follow-up strategies that keep momentum going and ensure that meetings translate into tangible results.

By the end of this chapter, you'll have a comprehensive understanding of how to transform meetings into motivating experiences that energize your team and drive success. You'll learn how to turn what might have once been seen as obligatory gatherings into strategic opportunities for innovation and collaboration.

As we embark on this journey to redefine meetings, keep in mind that the skills you've honed in communication and conflict resolution will serve you well. They are the building blocks upon which engaging and effective meetings are built. With these tools, you're ready to lead your team in meetings that matter, paving the way for enhanced productivity and stronger team dynamics.

So, let's dive in and explore how to make your meetings not just an agenda item but a highlight of your team's collaborative efforts. With the right approach, meetings can become a cornerstone of your leadership strategy, reinforcing your role as a motivational and effective leader.

- Designing Productive and Engaging Meetings

As we tackle the task of transforming meetings from obligatory affairs to dynamic powerhouses of productivity, let's start by examining the essential elements of planning and purpose. Meetings shouldn't be a mere checkbox on your weekly agenda; they should be strategically crafted gatherings where ideas converge, decisions are made, and progress is propelled. To achieve this, a meeting must have a clear purpose and a well-structured plan.

Think about meetings you've attended that left you questioning their necessity. Maybe they lacked focus, drifted off-topic, or concluded with more confusion than clarity. This is often the result of poor planning and undefined objectives. The Moron Manager, with his penchant for rambling meetings that lacked direction, left his team feeling scattered and disengaged. In contrast, the inspirational leader understood that a well-planned meeting could be a game-changer, using them as platforms to align teams and drive projects forward.

The first step in effective meeting planning is to define its purpose. Ask yourself: Why are we meeting? What do we need to achieve? Whether it's to brainstorm new ideas, resolve a specific issue, or provide project updates, having a clear goal will guide the meeting's structure and ensure that time is used efficiently. Without a defined purpose, meetings are prone to drift into aimless discussions and devolve into frustration.

Once the purpose is established, the next step is crafting an agenda. An agenda serves as a roadmap for the meeting, outlining topics for discussion and allocating time for each. It's a tool that helps keep the meeting focused, ensures that all necessary points are covered, and respects everyone's time. Share the agenda with participants ahead of time, allowing them to prepare and contribute meaningfully to the conversation. This preparation sets the stage for a more insightful and engaging dialogue.

Consider how you can design the meeting to encourage active participation. Think back to the inspirational leader who fostered a culture of open dialogue. Her meetings were characterized by an inclusive atmosphere where every participant felt empowered to share their insights. This wasn't by accident; it was the result of deliberate planning and facilitation.

To cultivate this environment, establish ground rules that promote respect and active listening. Encourage participants to voice their opinions and ask questions. Make it clear that all ideas are welcome and that diverse perspectives are valued. This approach not only enriches the discussion but also builds a sense of ownership and investment in the meeting's outcomes.

Incorporating interactive elements can also enhance engagement. This might include brainstorming sessions, breakout groups, or using technology to facilitate real-time feedback and collaboration. These techniques help maintain energy levels and ensure that meetings remain dynamic and productive.

My biggest success in getting people to be interactive in meetings is starting with a quiz. For an internal meeting it can be fun and related to the topic at hand in some way. For external meetings it can be a level set to see knowledge or thoughts on the topic before you begin. I have found that an online quiz that they can interact with and automatically does scoreboards is the best way to do this. Tools like Mentimeter are free and people can use their phones to interact.

Another crucial aspect of meeting planning is time management. We've all been in meetings that drag on longer than necessary, sapping energy and focus. To avoid this, allocate specific timeframes for each agenda item and stick to them. If a topic requires more discussion than anticipated, consider scheduling a follow-up meeting or assigning action items to delve deeper outside of the meeting. This discipline in time management ensures that meetings are concise and purposeful, respecting participants' schedules and maintaining momentum.

I've been in meetings where there was such poor time management that with a list of 3 things to do in a full day meeting, not a single item would be completed. In fact, we ended up with more topics than we started with! Unfortunately, the Moron Managers that were running these sessions wouldn't listen to the participants when we repeatedly requested more stringent time keeping and even suggested the structure on how to do this. The result? The meetings became less and less productive.

As the meeting progresses, keep an eye on the dynamics of the group. Be attuned to signs of disengagement or frustration and be prepared to adapt your approach if needed. Sometimes this means redirecting the conversation, inviting quieter participants to share their thoughts, or shifting focus if a topic isn't yielding productive dialogue. Flexibility, combined with a clear structure, allows you to steer the meeting toward its objective while maintaining a positive and collaborative atmosphere.

Why in those Moron Manager meetings did we end up going in circles or off on tangents? There was one particular Moron Manager who would feel the need to comment, advise and rant about every little thing that went through her head. She would argue with people on topics she had no experience on. She would take the discussion off in a completely different direction simply because she wasn't interested in the scheduled topic. She would try to undo decisions previously made simply because she didn't like the outcome (even if it didn't affect her team). In short, she made the meetings pointless. You can imagine how that made people feel. As a result, the meetings often got heated and even less productive.

The simple solution is really to ensure that only relevant people are in the meeting.

Remove those that aren't contributing or don't invite them in the first place. If they are so disruptive it is also worth tackling it with them directly (now that you know how to have difficult conversations!).

Lastly, prepare for the meeting's conclusion with a clear summary of decisions made and next steps. This closure not only reinforces the meeting's outcomes but also ensures accountability moving forward. Assign action items with specific deadlines and responsible parties, and confirm that everyone is aligned on what's expected. Maybe even repeat that quiz you did at the start to see if anyone's perspective or knowledge has changed?

By grounding your meetings in purpose and planning, you transform them from routine obligations into strategic opportunities. This shift not only enhances productivity but also strengthens team cohesion and morale. As we continue our exploration of productive meetings, we'll delve into techniques for encouraging participation and collaboration, ensuring every voice is heard and every meeting is a step toward achieving your team's goals.

With the right approach, your meetings can become more than just gatherings; they can be pivotal moments in your team's journey toward success. Let's continue to build on these foundations, equipping you with the skills to lead meetings that inspire, engage, and deliver tangible results.

- Encouraging Participation and Collaboration

Building on the solid foundation of purpose and planning, let's delve into the heart of what makes meetings truly meaningful: participation and collaboration. A meeting that simply disseminates information is a missed opportunity. Instead, meetings should be a forum for collective intelligence, where diverse ideas converge, and innovative solutions emerge. This is where the magic happens, where team members not only share their perspectives but build on each other's insights to create something greater than they could alone.

Think of meetings you've attended where the energy was palpable, where participants were engaged, ideas flowed freely, and everyone left feeling inspired to take action. These are the meetings that spark creativity and drive progress. The inspirational leader knew this well, transforming meetings into collaborative think tanks, where every participant felt valued and empowered to contribute.

Encouraging participation begins with setting the tone. A welcoming environment is crucial, one where everyone feels safe to express their ideas without fear of judgment or rejection. Establishing ground rules for respectful communication and active listening helps foster this atmosphere. Make it clear that every voice matters and that all contributions are valued, regardless of rank or role.

Start by inviting input from all participants. This can be as simple as going around the room for initial thoughts or using techniques like round-robin brainstorming to ensure everyone has an opportunity to speak. For those who may be hesitant to share in a group setting, consider collecting input in advance or using anonymous feedback tools to capture their insights. This inclusivity not only enriches the discussion but also builds a sense of ownership and investment in the meeting's outcomes.

Interactive elements can significantly boost engagement. Breakout groups can be particularly effective, allowing smaller clusters to dive deeper into specific topics before reconvening to share their findings with the larger group. This approach not only keeps energy levels high but also ensures that a variety of ideas are explored thoroughly.

Technology can also play a role in enhancing participation. Tools like digital whiteboards, real-time polls, and collaborative platforms enable participants to contribute in new and dynamic ways. These tools can be particularly useful in virtual or hybrid settings, ensuring that remote participants remain as engaged and involved as those in the room.

As a leader, your role is to facilitate collaboration, guiding the conversation and ensuring that it remains productive and focused. This means balancing the need for open dialogue with the agenda's objectives, encouraging quieter voices to speak up, and tactfully steering discussions back on track if they wander. Your ability to create a balanced and inclusive dialogue can transform a meeting from a routine exchange of information into an inspiring collaborative experience.

Consider the anecdote of the inspirational leader and her approach to meetings. She understood that the best ideas often come from unexpected places, and she made it a point to actively engage every participant. Her meetings were characterized by a dynamic interplay of ideas, where participants felt encouraged to challenge the status quo and explore new possibilities. This open, collaborative environment not only enriched the quality of the discussion but also reinforced the team's commitment to their shared goals.

But participation isn't just about talking—it's also about listening. Encourage active listening by modeling it yourself. Show that you're genuinely interested in what others have to say, ask follow-up questions, and acknowledge the contributions of each participant. This validates their input and encourages continued engagement.

Collaboration extends beyond the meeting itself. Encourage participants to follow up on the discussions, continue conversations, and collaborate on action items. Set up channels, whether through digital platforms or regular check-ins, to facilitate ongoing collaboration and idea sharing. This not only maintains momentum but also reinforces the meeting's impact, ensuring that discussions translate into meaningful action.

Lastly, celebrate collaborative successes. Acknowledge when teamwork leads to innovative solutions or significant progress, recognizing both individual contributions and the collective effort. This reinforcement not only boosts morale but also encourages continued collaboration in future meetings.

Through thoughtful facilitation and a focus on participation and collaboration, you transform meetings into vibrant hubs of creativity and innovation. These sessions become more than just a gathering of people—they become a powerful catalyst for progress and engagement, driving your team toward their goals.

As we move forward, we'll explore how to ensure that the momentum built in meetings translates into actionable results through effective follow-up and accountability. With these skills, you're well on your way to leading meetings that are not only productive but also inspiring, reinforcing your role as a motivational leader. Let's continue this journey, equipping you with the tools to make every meeting a meaningful and impactful experience.

- Meeting Follow-Up: Ensuring Accountability and Progress

As we bring our exploration of transforming meetings to a close, let's focus on the crucial final step: ensuring that the energy and ideas generated during meetings translate into tangible results through effective follow-up and accountability. You've set the stage with purpose, engaged participants with collaboration, and now it's time to harness that momentum, ensuring that the outcomes of your meetings propel your team forward.

Reflect on meetings where great ideas were born, but without clear follow-up, they vanished into the ether, leaving participants wondering what came of their contributions. The Moron Manager often failed in this area, conducting meetings that ended with a vague sense of resolution but no concrete steps, leaving his team adrift. In contrast, the inspirational leader made sure her meetings were the starting point for action, not the end, ensuring accountability and progress.

The first step in effective follow-up is documenting the meeting's outcomes. This involves capturing key decisions, action items, timelines, and responsibilities. Make this documentation accessible to all participants soon after the meeting. This not only reinforces what was discussed and decided but also serves as a reference point for future actions and accountability.

Assign clear action items with specific deadlines and responsible parties. Ambiguity is the enemy of progress. Ensure that everyone knows what's expected of them and by when. This clarity helps prevent misunderstandings and ensures that all team members are aligned in their efforts.

Regular check-ins and updates are crucial for maintaining momentum. Depending on the scope of the action items, these might be brief weekly updates, more detailed monthly reviews, or even project-specific meetings.

These touchpoints provide an opportunity to review progress, address any roadblocks, and adjust plans as necessary. They also reinforce accountability, as team members know they will be expected to report on their progress.

Encourage a culture of accountability within your team. This doesn't mean micromanaging every task, but rather fostering a sense of ownership and commitment to the team's shared goals. Recognize and celebrate achievements, both individual and collective, to reinforce the value of accountability and motivate continued effort.

Consider the inspirational leader's approach to following up on meetings. Her commitment to accountability was evident in the way she empowered her team to take ownership of their tasks. She provided the support and resources they needed, but she also trusted them to deliver on their commitments. This balance of support and autonomy not only drove results but also enhanced the team's sense of agency and pride in their work.

Feedback is another important element of follow-up. Encourage open dialogue about what's working and what's not. This feedback loop helps you refine your meeting processes, ensuring they remain effective and responsive to your team's needs. It also reinforces a culture of continuous improvement, where learning and adaptation are integral to success.

In the context of virtual or hybrid meetings, these principles are even more critical. With team members potentially dispersed across locations and time zones, clear documentation, regular updates, and effective communication become the glue that holds projects together. Use technology to your advantage, leveraging collaborative platforms to keep everyone connected and informed.

The ultimate goal of meetings is to drive action and results, but this requires a strategic approach to follow-up. By ensuring accountability and maintaining momentum, you transform meetings from isolated events into integral components of your team's success. Meetings become more than just a time to talk—they become a catalyst for meaningful progress and achievement.

As we wrap up this chapter on transforming meetings, reflect on the insights gained and how they can be applied to your leadership practice. Meetings are a powerful tool when used effectively, capable of energizing your team, fostering collaboration, and driving results. With the skills and strategies covered here, you're well-equipped to lead meetings that are both productive and inspiring.

Our journey now leads us to the next chapter, where we will explore how to cultivate future leaders through coaching and mentoring. Building on the foundation of effective meetings, you'll learn how to nurture the next generation of talent, empowering them to achieve their potential and contribute to your team's success. As you continue this journey, take with you the knowledge and confidence gained here, ready to lead with purpose and inspire those around you.

Chapter 6: Cultivating Future Leaders: Coaching and Mentoring

As we step into the world of cultivating future leaders, the focus shifts from immediate tasks and team dynamics to the long-term vision of mentorship and growth. This chapter is dedicated to the noble endeavor of coaching and mentoring—a pivotal component of inspirational leadership. Here, we explore how to nurture the next generation of talent, empowering them to reach their full potential and contribute meaningfully to the success of your team and organization.

Consider the leaders who have left a lasting impact on your career. What set them apart? Often, it's not merely their skills or achievements, but their willingness to invest in your development, to guide you through challenges, and to celebrate your successes as if they were their own. These are the leaders who see potential where others see tasks, who understand that their legacy is built not just on their accomplishments but on the leaders they've helped shape.

In the same vein, think about the Moron Manager, who was so mired in micromanagement and self-interest that he missed opportunities to cultivate his team's potential. His short-sightedness created an environment of stagnation rather than growth. I've actually worked with managers whose attitude was that growth and development was something you do in your spare time!

One Moron Manager also used to publicly complain about what people chose to do in their spare time with statements like "why are they learning Turkish or the violin when they should be doing work related learning?". She had the attitude that people should prioritize work above all else. The result of this lack of coaching and mentorship and this standoffish attitude? A workforce who didn't grow or develop and a company product that got gradually worse and worse as a result.

In contrast, the inspirational leader recognized the importance of mentorship, fostering an environment where learning and development were not just encouraged but expected. The leader who actively encourages their team to block off an hour or so a week to work on self-development. The result? A team that learns and grows. A team that brings new ideas to the table. A team that naturally increases their confidence and productivity.

The goal of this chapter is to equip you with the tools and insights needed to become a mentor who inspires and empowers. We'll delve into the nuances of identifying and nurturing rising stars, exploring effective coaching techniques, and understanding the long-term benefits of investing in your team's growth.

At the heart of mentorship lies the ability to see and support potential. It's about recognizing the unique strengths and aspirations of each team member and providing them with the opportunities and guidance they need to flourish. This begins with active observation and engagement, getting to know your team on a deeper level, and understanding what drives them.

Creating a culture of mentorship involves more than just formal programs; it's about embedding development into the everyday operations of your team. It's about fostering an environment where asking questions, seeking feedback, and taking on new challenges are integral to the team's ethos. We'll explore strategies for integrating coaching into your leadership practice, ensuring that every interaction becomes an opportunity for growth.

Effective mentoring also requires a willingness to share your knowledge and experiences openly. It's about being transparent about your own journey—the successes as well as the missteps—and using those lessons to guide others. This vulnerability not only builds trust but also reinforces the idea that learning is a continuous process, one that extends throughout a career.

As we delve into this chapter, consider how you can apply these principles in your leadership journey. Reflect on the mentors who have shaped your path and think about the legacy you want to leave. By investing in the growth of others, you not only create a stronger, more capable team but also enhance your own leadership skills, reinforcing your impact as an inspirational leader.

In the coming sections, we'll explore practical techniques for coaching and mentoring, focusing on how to create meaningful development opportunities and foster an environment of trust and support. With these insights, you'll be well-equipped to guide your team toward their professional goals, ensuring that they are ready to take on the challenges of tomorrow.

So, let's embark on this journey of mentorship, ready to shape the future by empowering those around us. As we delve into the art of coaching and mentoring, we'll reinforce the foundation of trust and collaboration that's been built throughout this book, setting the stage for a legacy of leadership that transcends individual achievements.

- Identifying and Nurturing Rising Stars

As we dive into the art of mentorship, let's begin with the vital task of identifying and nurturing rising stars within your team. The future of any organization depends on its ability to cultivate talent, to recognize potential where others might see only present skills. By pinpointing those who can grow into leadership roles, you pave the way for a thriving, resilient team ready to tackle whatever challenges come their way.

Picture the times when a manager saw something in you that perhaps even you hadn't recognized yet. Their belief and investment in your potential not only elevated your performance but also instilled a sense of confidence and loyalty. Now think of the Moron Manager, who, in his short-sightedness, overlooked the budding talents of his team, stifling innovation and growth in the process.

Identifying rising stars begins with observation and engagement. Spend time understanding the strengths, weaknesses, and aspirations of each team member. This isn't about playing favorites or placing undue pressure on individuals but about recognizing those who show the initiative, adaptability, and drive that are hallmarks of potential leaders.

Look for qualities such as curiosity, resilience, and the ability to collaborate effectively. Rising stars are often those who ask insightful questions, who aren't afraid to step outside their comfort zones, and who show a willingness to take on new challenges. They're the team members who consistently seek feedback and strive for improvement, demonstrating that learning is a lifelong journey.

Once identified, the next step is nurturing that potential. This involves creating an environment where growth is not just possible but encouraged. Provide opportunities for these individuals to stretch their skills and expand their experiences. This might include leading projects, participating in cross-functional teams, or exploring roles in different areas of the organization. By challenging them to step up and take on new responsibilities, you help them develop the confidence and capabilities they need to thrive.

Feedback is a critical component of this growth process. Provide regular, constructive feedback that guides their development and reinforces their progress. Focus on both strengths and areas for improvement, ensuring your feedback is specific, actionable, and grounded in genuine support. This approach not only helps them hone their skills but also reinforces the trust and rapport that are essential to effective mentorship.

Consider the techniques used by the inspirational leader who prioritized the development of her team. She understood that growth wasn't a linear path but a dynamic process that required nurturing and patience. Her approach was to tailor her mentorship to the individual, recognizing that each person's journey was unique. By doing so, she created a culture where development was embedded in the team's DNA, fueling both personal and professional growth.

Mentoring rising stars also involves sharing your own experiences—the triumphs and the setbacks. Be open about your journey, the lessons learned, and the obstacles overcome. This transparency not only builds credibility but also humanizes the path to leadership, showing that it's okay to stumble along the way as long as you get back up and continue moving forward.

It's also important to celebrate their achievements, both big and small. Recognize when they've overcome a challenge, met a goal, or contributed meaningfully to the team's success. This acknowledgment not only boosts morale but also reinforces their sense of belonging and commitment to the team.

Don't forget to encourage peer mentorship as well. Foster an environment where team members support and learn from each other, creating a network of shared knowledge and experience. By encouraging this collaborative approach, you not only strengthen individual growth but also enhance team cohesion and resilience.

Finally, remember that mentorship is a two-way street. While you're guiding and supporting their development, be open to the insights and fresh perspectives they bring to the table. These rising stars are the future of your organization, and their ideas and innovations can drive meaningful change.

As we move forward in this chapter, we'll explore practical coaching techniques to further support your mentorship journey. With these tools, you'll be equipped to guide your team members as they step into their potential, ensuring that they are prepared to lead with confidence and purpose. Let's continue this

journey of empowerment, creating a legacy of
leadership that inspires and uplifts.

- Effective Coaching Techniques for Development

Having set the stage for identifying and nurturing rising stars, it's time to delve into the practical techniques of coaching. Coaching is less about telling and more about guiding, less about dictating and more about facilitating. It's about helping individuals discover their own solutions and grow into their potential. Effective coaching empowers team members to take ownership of their development, fostering independence and confidence.

Consider the role of a coach in sports. They don't play the game for the athletes; instead, they provide guidance, feedback, and support, enabling their players to perform at their best. Similarly, in a professional setting, your role as a coach is to inspire, challenge, and support your team members, helping them navigate their path with confidence and clarity.

One of the foundational techniques in coaching is asking powerful questions. These are open-ended questions that encourage reflection and self-discovery. Instead of providing answers, ask questions that prompt your team members to think critically and explore different perspectives. Questions like, "What do you think is the best approach to this challenge?" or "How do you envision the outcome of this project?" empower individuals to take control of their development and find their own solutions.

Active listening is equally important in the coaching process. This means giving your full attention, showing genuine interest in their responses, and being present in the conversation. Listening not only helps you understand their challenges and aspirations but also validates their experiences and builds trust. It shows that you value their input and are committed to supporting their growth.

Feedback is another crucial component of effective coaching. However, it's important to approach feedback as a dialogue rather than a monologue. Encourage a two-way conversation where team members feel comfortable sharing their perspectives and asking for clarification. This collaborative approach fosters open communication and mutual respect, reinforcing the coaching relationship.

When providing feedback, focus on behavior rather than personality. Be specific and constructive, highlighting both strengths and areas for improvement. Use real examples to illustrate your points, and provide actionable suggestions for development. This method ensures that feedback is not only informative but also practical and immediately applicable.

Goal setting is another powerful coaching technique. Work with your team members to establish clear, achievable goals that align with their personal aspirations and the team's objectives. These goals should be specific, measurable, attainable, relevant, and time-bound (SMART) to ensure clarity and accountability. By setting meaningful goals, you help individuals focus their efforts and measure their progress, providing a sense of direction and purpose.

Encourage self-reflection as part of the coaching process. Regularly ask your team members to reflect on their experiences, successes, and challenges. What did they learn from a particular project? What could they have done differently? This reflection not only enhances self-awareness but also promotes continuous learning and growth.

Consider the inspirational leader who used coaching as a cornerstone of her leadership practice. She understood that each team member was on a unique journey, and she tailored her coaching approach to suit their individual needs. By asking insightful questions, providing constructive feedback, and encouraging goal setting, she fostered an environment where growth was not just a goal but a reality.

Balancing challenge and support is key in coaching. While it's important to challenge your team members to step outside their comfort zones and take on new responsibilities, it's equally important to provide the support and resources they need to succeed. This balance ensures that individuals feel confident in their abilities while still pushing themselves to grow and develop.

Lastly, remember that coaching is an ongoing process. It's not a one-time event but a continuous journey of learning and development. Regular check-ins and progress reviews help maintain momentum and reinforce accountability. Celebrate achievements along the way, recognizing both the individual's efforts and the impact on the team's success.

As we continue to explore the theme of mentorship, the next section will focus on fostering an environment that supports long-term success and growth. With these coaching techniques, you'll be well-equipped to guide your team members as they navigate their professional journeys, ensuring they are prepared to lead with confidence and purpose. Let's continue this journey of empowerment, building a legacy of leadership that inspires and uplifts.

- Mentoring for Long-Term Success and Growth

As we wrap up our journey through the art of mentorship, it's time to focus on creating a long-term environment that supports sustained growth and success. Building a culture of mentorship within your team or organization is about more than just individual development; it's about creating a legacy of continuous learning and leadership that endures beyond your tenure.

Reflect on the environments that have allowed you to thrive. Chances are, these weren't places where mentorship was a one-off effort, but where growth was embedded into the very fabric of the team. It's about cultivating conditions where everyone feels empowered to learn, contribute, and evolve.

To establish such an environment, it starts with leadership commitment. As a leader, you set the tone for a culture of growth and mentorship. This means demonstrating your own commitment to learning and development, being open about your own journey, and showing a willingness to grow alongside your team. This openness reinforces the idea that learning is a shared endeavor.

Encouraging a growth mindset is critical. This mindset, popularized by psychologist Carol Dweck, emphasizes the belief that abilities and intelligence can be developed through dedication and hard work. It's about viewing challenges as opportunities to grow and learning from setbacks. When your team adopts a growth mindset, they're more likely to embrace new challenges, persist through difficulties, and support each other's development.

To nurture a growth mindset, celebrate effort and progress, not just outcomes. Recognize the hard work and perseverance your team demonstrates, even if the desired results aren't immediately achieved. This acknowledgement encourages risk-taking and innovation, essential components of continuous growth and learning.

Fostering a culture of feedback is another important aspect. Create an environment where feedback flows freely and constructively, both from leaders to team members and among peers. This openness helps team members identify areas for improvement and develop their skills, while also reinforcing a sense of trust and collaboration.

Consider the inspirational leader who made feedback an integral part of her team's culture. She encouraged regular feedback exchanges, embracing both formal reviews and informal check-ins. This approach not only helped individuals grow but also strengthened the team's cohesion and resilience.

Providing opportunities for continuous learning is also vital. Encourage your team to pursue professional development through workshops, courses, and conferences. Support cross-training and job rotation to widen skill sets and perspectives. Facilitate access to resources and networks that can inspire and enhance their development.

Mentorship shouldn't be a one-way street. Encourage peer-to-peer mentoring, where team members share their knowledge and experience with each other. This collaborative approach not only enhances learning but also builds stronger connections and a more cohesive team dynamic.

Support informal mentoring relationships by creating spaces and opportunities for these interactions to occur. Whether it's through lunch-and-learns, team-building events, or mentorship circles, these informal settings can foster organic mentoring relationships that complement formal programs.

As you cultivate this environment, remember that mentorship is a long-term commitment. It's about consistently reinforcing the values of learning, collaboration, and growth. Regularly assess the effectiveness of your mentorship efforts and be open to making adjustments as needed. This adaptability ensures that your mentorship culture remains relevant and impactful.

As we transition to the next chapter, which will explore strategies for avoiding common management pitfalls, carry forward the insights and strategies gleaned from nurturing future leaders. Mentorship and leadership are deeply intertwined, and the skills developed here will enhance your ability to lead effectively and inspire those around you.

By embedding mentorship into the core of your leadership practice, you're not only empowering your team to reach their potential but also creating a lasting legacy of growth and development. With a commitment to mentorship, you cultivate leaders who are ready to face the challenges of tomorrow, ensuring the continued success of your team and organization. As we move forward, let's keep this spirit of mentorship alive, paving the way for a brighter, more empowered future.

Chapter 7: Avoiding Common Management Pitfalls

As we turn our attention to navigating the common pitfalls of management, it's important to acknowledge that every leader, no matter how seasoned, encounters challenges along the way. The key lies not in avoiding mistakes altogether—an impossible feat—but in recognizing them early and responding with openness and adaptability. This chapter is dedicated to equipping you with the insights and strategies needed to steer clear of these pitfalls, allowing you to lead with clarity and confidence.

Consider moments when things didn't go as planned, when the best intentions were met with unexpected obstacles. Perhaps you've seen a leader stumble into micromanagement, inadvertently stifling creativity and autonomy. Or recall the Moron Manager, so entrenched in his outdated ways that he missed opportunities for innovation and growth. In contrast, the inspirational leader embraced challenges as learning opportunities, adapting her approach and fostering an environment of resilience and growth.

The aim of this chapter is to help you identify and overcome the traps that can derail even the most well-intentioned leaders. We'll explore the dynamics of micromanagement, the balance between control and empowerment, and the importance of maintaining an open and adaptable mindset. By mastering these elements, you'll be better prepared to lead your team effectively and inspire them to reach new heights.

Micromanagement is one of the most common pitfalls, often born from a desire to ensure success. However, this approach can undermine morale and stifle innovation. We'll discuss ways to recognize the signs of micromanagement and explore strategies to empower your team, fostering trust and autonomy while ensuring accountability.

Balancing control and empowerment is another critical area. It's about setting clear expectations and providing the support needed to achieve them without overshadowing your team's capabilities. We'll delve into techniques for establishing this balance, allowing for both independence and guidance within your team.

Finally, we'll explore the necessity of maintaining an open-minded and adaptable approach. The business landscape is ever-changing, and leaders must be willing to embrace new ideas and adapt to evolving circumstances. We'll highlight the importance of remaining curious and flexible, continually seeking opportunities for improvement and growth.

As you engage with these themes, reflect on your own experiences and how they've shaped your leadership journey. Recognize the growth that comes from learning through challenges and the strength that lies in overcoming them. By preparing for these common pitfalls, you're not only enhancing your leadership skills but also reinforcing your ability to inspire and uplift your team.

As we explore these potential pitfalls and their solutions, take with you the lessons from previous chapters on communication, mentorship, and team dynamics. These foundational skills will serve as your compass, guiding you through the complexities of leadership and helping you build a legacy of empowerment and success.

In the sections that follow, we'll delve deeper into each of these common pitfalls, providing practical strategies to navigate them effectively. With these insights, you'll be well-equipped to lead with confidence and resilience, ensuring that your leadership journey is both impactful and rewarding. Let's begin this exploration of potential challenges, ready to transform them into opportunities for growth and development.

- Recognizing and Overcoming Micromanagement Tendencies

As we delve into the intricacies of avoiding common management pitfalls, let's begin with a trap that ensnares many well-meaning leaders: micromanagement. It's an easy cycle to slip into, often disguised as a desire to ensure quality and success. Yet, while the intention might be good, micromanagement can severely undermine both the morale and productivity of a team. Understanding how to identify and break free from this pattern is key to fostering a thriving work environment.

Think of times when you've felt overly scrutinized, where every decision, no matter how minor, had to be approved by a manager. The result is often a stifled sense of autonomy, where creativity is squashed, and initiative feels more like a risk than an opportunity.

The Moron Manager excelled in this area, demanding control over every detail, which left his team feeling demoralized and untrusted. It meant the team didn't offer any solutions – after all what's the point when they will come in and tell you how to do it anyway? On the other hand, the inspirational leader struck a balance between oversight and freedom, empowering her team to bring their best ideas to the table.

To combat micromanagement, start by examining the root causes. Often, it stems from a lack of trust or a fear of failure. As leaders, it's crucial to recognize when these feelings are influencing management style and to address them head-on. Building trust within your team is foundational to moving away from micromanagement.

This trust starts with clear communication and setting expectations. When your team knows what is expected and understands the goals, they are more likely to take ownership of their work and deliver results.

Developing clear and comprehensive guidelines can help. These serve as a framework within which your team can operate independently. Set boundaries around when decisions need managerial input and when team members can act autonomously. This clarity not only empowers your team but also alleviates the pressure on you to oversee every detail.

Encouraging autonomy means providing the resources and support your team needs to succeed. Ensure they have access to the tools, training, and information necessary to carry out their responsibilities. Be available for guidance and support but resist the urge to intervene unless absolutely necessary. This balance helps team members feel empowered and trusted, while still knowing they have support when needed.

Regular, focused check-ins can replace the need for constant oversight. Use these meetings to discuss progress, address challenges, and offer guidance while allowing your team to take the lead in finding solutions. This approach not only respects their autonomy but also fosters a collaborative environment where team members feel valued and motivated.

Feedback plays a crucial role in overcoming micromanagement. Encourage open dialogue where team members feel comfortable sharing their thoughts and ideas. This two-way communication fosters trust and helps you gauge when to step back and when to offer more support. It also reinforces a culture where everyone's input is valued and considered.

Consider the transformational impact of the inspirational leader's approach. By relinquishing some control and trusting her team, she enabled them to innovate and take initiative, resulting in a more engaged and productive work environment. Her team felt empowered to take risks and explore new solutions, knowing they had the freedom to make decisions within a supportive framework.

Another effective strategy is to focus on outcomes rather than processes. Instead of dictating how tasks should be completed, concentrate on the desired results. This shift in focus allows team members to use their expertise and creativity to find the best path forward, fostering a sense of ownership and pride in their work.

Remember, avoiding micromanagement doesn't mean disengaging or abdicating responsibility. It's about finding the right balance between providing guidance and allowing independence. By empowering your team, you're not only enhancing their development but also freeing up your time to focus on the bigger picture of leadership.

As we continue exploring common management pitfalls, our next focus will be on balancing control with empowerment, a crucial aspect that complements the battle against micromanagement. With these insights, you'll be well-equipped to create a work environment where your team feels motivated, trusted, and capable of achieving great results. Let's continue this journey, ready to build a leadership style that inspires and uplifts.

Balancing Control with Empowerment

In the quest to maintain a harmonious balance between control and empowerment, we find the sweet spot of effective leadership. It's a delicate dance, one that requires both intuition and strategy. While control ensures alignment and consistency, empowerment drives innovation and engagement. Striking this balance not only enhances team performance but also fosters a culture of trust and mutual respect.

Reflect on the times when a manager either held the reins too tightly or let them slacken excessively. The Moron Manager often swung between these extremes, either suffocating creativity with overbearing control or leaving his team in a lurch with vague directives. In contrast, the inspirational leader mastered the art of balancing control with empowerment, allowing her team to thrive within a well-defined framework.

To strike this balance, begin with establishing a strong foundation of trust. Trust is the bridge between control and empowerment. It allows you to step back and let your team take the lead, knowing they'll deliver on their commitments. Building this trust starts with setting clear, achievable goals and communicating them effectively. When your team understands the vision and their role in achieving it, they're more likely to feel motivated and aligned.

Clarity in roles and expectations is equally important. Clearly defined roles help prevent confusion and overlap, ensuring that everyone knows their responsibilities and can work independently towards common goals. This clarity empowers team members to make decisions within their scope, while still feeling supported and aligned with the team's objectives.

Another key aspect is providing the right level of oversight. This doesn't mean micromanaging every task, but rather offering guidance and support where needed. Regular check-ins and feedback sessions can help you gauge how much oversight is required and adjust accordingly. This approach not only maintains alignment but also reinforces your team's autonomy and capabilities.

Encouraging decision-making within defined boundaries is another effective strategy. Set clear parameters within which your team can operate independently, and trust them to make decisions that align with these boundaries. This approach allows for creativity and innovation while ensuring that actions remain consistent with the team's goals.

Feedback is a powerful tool in maintaining this balance. Encourage open communication where team members feel comfortable sharing their ideas and concerns. This dialogue provides valuable insights into how your team is functioning and allows you to adjust your approach as needed. It also reinforces a culture of continuous improvement, where feedback is seen as a means of growth rather than criticism.

Consider the impact of the inspirational leader's approach to balancing control and empowerment. By providing her team with the freedom to explore and innovate within a supportive framework, she created an environment where creativity flourished and results were consistently delivered. Her ability to adapt her leadership style based on the needs of her team enabled both her and her team to excel.

Remember that balancing control with empowerment is not a static process—it requires ongoing evaluation and adjustment. As your team grows and evolves, so too should your leadership approach. Remain open to feedback and be willing to adapt as circumstances change. This flexibility is crucial in maintaining a dynamic and engaged team environment.

In fostering this balance, it's important to recognize that empowerment is not synonymous with abdication. It's about providing the resources, guidance, and support your team needs to succeed while trusting them to take the initiative and ownership of their work. This trust not only enhances their development but also reinforces their commitment to the team's success.

As we continue our exploration of common management pitfalls, our final focus will be on remaining open-minded and adaptable. This mindset is essential in navigating the complexities of leadership and ensuring your team can thrive in an ever-changing landscape. With these insights, you'll be well-prepared to lead with confidence, fostering an environment where your team feels empowered and motivated to achieve great results. Let's move forward, ready to embrace the challenges and opportunities that lie ahead.

- Remaining Open-Minded and Adaptable

As we draw our exploration of common management pitfalls to a close, let's turn our focus to cultivating an open-minded and adaptable approach to leadership. In today's ever-evolving business environment, change is a constant companion. The leaders who thrive are those who embrace flexibility and curiosity, continually seeking new perspectives and solutions. This mindset not only enhances personal growth but also fosters a culture of innovation and resilience within your team.

Think of the leaders who have inspired you with their adaptability, their ability to pivot in the face of challenges and seize opportunities others might overlook. The Moron Manager, in his rigid adherence to outdated methods, often missed these chances, leaving his team stuck in a cycle of stagnation. In contrast, the inspirational leader viewed each challenge as an opportunity to learn and grow, adapting her strategies to meet the needs of her team and the demands of the market.

The journey to becoming an open-minded and adaptable leader begins with self-awareness. Recognize your own biases and limitations, and actively seek to expand your understanding. This means welcoming diverse perspectives and being willing to question your assumptions. By embracing this mindset, you open the door to new ideas and innovations that can propel your team forward.

Encourage a culture of learning and experimentation within your team. Create an environment where team members feel safe to explore new ideas and challenge the status quo. This doesn't mean pursuing change for the sake of change, but rather fostering an atmosphere where calculated risks are encouraged, and learning is prioritized. Celebrate both successes and failures, recognizing that each is an opportunity for growth.

Adaptability also requires a willingness to change course when necessary. This might mean reevaluating strategies, revisiting goals, or redefining roles as circumstances evolve. Be transparent with your team about the reasons for these changes and how they align with the broader vision. This openness not only builds trust but also reinforces the shared commitment to the team's success.

Consider the inspirational leader's approach to adaptability. She understood that flexibility was not a weakness but a strength, allowing her team to navigate challenges with confidence and creativity. Her openness to new ideas and willingness to adjust her strategies cultivated a team that was not only resilient but also innovative and engaged.

Remain open to feedback from your team and be willing to adjust your leadership style based on their needs. This two-way communication strengthens relationships and ensures that you're providing the support and guidance necessary for your team to thrive. It also reinforces a culture of continuous improvement, where everyone is committed to learning and growth.

Empower your team to take ownership of their development and encourage them to seek out learning opportunities both within and outside the organization. This proactive approach not only enhances their skills but also reinforces their sense of agency and commitment to the team's success.

As we conclude this chapter, reflect on the insights and strategies we've explored. By avoiding the pitfalls of micromanagement, balancing control with empowerment, and maintaining an open-minded and adaptable approach, you're well-equipped to lead your team with confidence and resilience. These skills not only enhance your leadership effectiveness but also foster a culture of trust, innovation, and collaboration.

In preparing for the final chapter, where we'll focus on embracing a positive leadership journey, carry forward the lessons learned here. The ability to navigate challenges with an open mind and a flexible approach is integral to building a lasting legacy of leadership. With these insights, you're ready to inspire and empower your team, ensuring their continued growth and success.

Let's move into the final chapter with a renewed commitment to leading with heart, adaptability, and vision. As we delve into embracing the journey of leadership, keep in mind that each step you take is an opportunity to learn, grow, and make a meaningful impact on those you lead. Let's continue this journey together, ready to create a brighter and more empowered future.

Chapter 8: Conclusion: Embracing a Positive Leadership Journey

- Continual Growth and Development as a Leader

As we embark on the final leg of our journey through the art of effective management, it's time to reflect on the path we've traversed and embrace the ongoing voyage of leadership with renewed purpose and positivity. This chapter is dedicated to the concept of continual growth and the legacy you leave as a leader. It's about recognizing that leadership is not a destination but a dynamic, ever-evolving process.

Think back to the leaders who have left an indelible mark on your career. It wasn't just their decisions or strategies that made an impact, but the way they embraced the journey itself—constantly learning, adapting, and inspiring. These leaders understood that their influence extended far beyond daily tasks or quarterly results; it was about fostering a culture of growth and resilience that resonated throughout their teams.

In contrast, consider the Moron Manager, whose stagnant approach and reluctance to adapt left his team feeling unfulfilled and undervalued. His lack of vision and unwillingness to embrace change stifled potential and missed opportunities for growth. On the flip side, the inspirational leader approached her role with an open heart and an inquisitive mind, always seeking ways to uplift her team and enhance their collective journey.

The goal of this chapter is to equip you with the mindset and strategies needed to continue your leadership journey with intention and optimism. We'll explore the importance of self-reflection and the value of setting future leadership goals. By embracing this mindset, you'll not only enhance your own growth but also inspire those around you to reach new heights.

Self-reflection is a critical component of embracing the journey. It involves regularly assessing your leadership style, the impact of your decisions, and the growth of your team. This reflection provides valuable insights into what's working well and where there might be room for improvement. By taking the time to reflect, you reinforce a culture of continuous learning, both for yourself and your team.

Setting future leadership goals is another essential step. These goals should be ambitious yet achievable, aligned with both your personal aspirations and the needs of your team. They serve as a roadmap for your leadership journey, providing direction and purpose while allowing for flexibility and adaptation as circumstances evolve.

Consider the inspirational leader's approach to embracing her leadership journey. Her commitment to reflection and goal-setting not only enhanced her personal growth but also reinforced her team's development. By sharing her journey openly, she fostered a culture of transparency and trust, empowering her team to embrace their own paths with confidence and enthusiasm.

As we delve into this final chapter, remember that leadership is a shared journey. It's about creating a legacy that transcends individual achievements and inspires others to continue the path you've set. By embracing this mindset, you're not only enriching your own experience but also contributing to a brighter, more empowered future for your team and organization.

With these insights, let's step into the final chapter, ready to embrace the positive journey of leadership. As we explore the themes of growth, reflection, and legacy, carry with you the lessons learned throughout this book. Together, we'll reinforce the foundation of effective management and inspire a new generation of leaders to reach their full potential. Let's embark on this final chapter with optimism and purpose, ready to create a lasting impact on those we lead.

- Continual Growth and Development as a Leader

As we step into the final chapter, let's begin with one of the most profound aspects of leadership: the power of self-reflection. It's a tool that serves leaders by illuminating pathways to growth, offering clarity in decision-making, and fostering a deeper understanding of oneself and one's impact. In the hustle and bustle of daily management, it's easy to overlook the importance of pausing and reflecting, yet it is this very pause that can transform a good leader into a great one.

Think back to moments in your career where a bit of introspection could have changed the course of events—a chance to reconsider an approach, to acknowledge a misstep, or to recognize a triumph that otherwise might have gone unnoticed. Consider the Moron Manager, who seldom paused for reflection, plowing ahead without regard for the lessons of experience. His leadership was reactive rather than proactive, leaving little room for learning or growth. In contrast, the inspirational leader dedicated time to self-reflection, using it as a compass to guide her actions and decisions, continually evolving her leadership style in response to insights gained.

Self-reflection begins with the simple act of asking yourself the right questions. What worked well in that situation? What could have been handled differently? How did my actions affect the team? This inquiry isn't about self-criticism but about understanding and growth. It's about acknowledging both successes and failures as opportunities to learn and improve.

To make self-reflection a habit, schedule regular time for it. Whether it's weekly, monthly, or after significant projects, setting aside time to reflect ensures it becomes a consistent part of your leadership practice. During these sessions, review your goals, assess your progress, and consider any adjustments that might be needed. This ongoing evaluation keeps you aligned with your vision and responsive to the dynamic needs of your team.

Journaling can be a powerful tool in this process. Writing down your thoughts and reflections not only helps clarify your thinking but also provides a valuable record of your journey. Over time, reviewing past entries can reveal patterns, highlight growth, and reinforce learning, offering a tangible testament to your development as a leader.

Feedback from others is also an essential element of self-reflection. Encourage honest and constructive feedback from your team, peers, and mentors. This external perspective can provide insights you might not see yourself and can help identify areas for further growth. By embracing feedback, you demonstrate openness and a commitment to continuous improvement, reinforcing a culture of transparency and trust.

Consider the inspirational leader's approach to self-reflection. She regularly sought feedback from her team, using it to inform her self-reflection and guide her development. Her willingness to learn from others not only enhanced her leadership effectiveness but also modeled the value of feedback and reflection for her team.

Self-reflection is not just about looking inward; it's also about looking forward. Use your reflections to set future leadership goals that align with your personal aspirations and the needs of your team. These goals should be specific, measurable, and adaptable, providing a clear path for your ongoing development while allowing for flexibility as circumstances evolve.

As you cultivate the habit of self-reflection, remember that it's a journey, not a destination. It's about embracing your leadership path with an open heart and a curious mind, continually seeking to learn and grow. By making reflection a core component of your leadership practice, you not only enhance your effectiveness but also inspire those around you to do the same.

As we continue through this final chapter, our focus will shift to setting and pursuing future leadership goals. With the insights gained from self-reflection, you'll be well-equipped to navigate this process, ensuring that your leadership journey is both fulfilling and impactful. Let's move forward with a renewed commitment to growth and learning, ready to create a legacy of leadership that inspires and uplifts.

- Building a Legacy of Inspirational Leadership

Building on the foundation of self-reflection, we now turn our attention to setting and pursuing future leadership goals. Goal setting is not simply about charting a course for personal or professional advancement; it's about crafting a vision that aligns with your values, inspires your team, and contributes to the broader mission of your organization. Thoughtful goal setting serves as both a beacon and a roadmap, guiding you through the complexities and opportunities of leadership.

Imagine the difference between a journey embarked upon with a clear destination and one without. The Moron Manager, unfocused and directionless, often found himself lost in the weeds of day-to-day tasks, lacking clear objectives that could drive meaningful progress.

In stark contrast, the inspirational leader set goals that were ambitious yet attainable, using them as a compass to navigate challenges and seize opportunities. Her goals not only propelled her forward but also inspired her team to strive for excellence.

The first step in effective goal setting is clarity. Define what you want to achieve and why it matters, both to you and your team. Your goals should be specific and measurable, providing a clear target to aim for and a means of tracking progress. This specificity not only clarifies your intentions but also allows you to celebrate milestones along the way, reinforcing motivation and commitment.

Align your goals with your core values and the mission of your organization. When goals resonate with your values, they hold more significance and are more likely to inspire sustained effort. This alignment also ensures that your goals support the broader objectives of your team and organization, contributing to a cohesive and collaborative pursuit of success.

Consider the strategic elements of goal setting. Break larger goals into smaller, manageable steps that provide clear direction and allow for incremental progress. This approach not only makes daunting goals more achievable but also creates a sense of momentum as each step is completed. Establish timelines for each phase, ensuring that progress is consistent and aligned with your overall vision.

Flexibility is crucial in goal setting. While it's important to have a clear direction, remain open to adjusting your goals as circumstances evolve. The business landscape is ever-changing, and leaders must be willing to adapt their plans to meet new challenges and seize emerging opportunities. This adaptability ensures that your goals remain relevant and impactful.

As you pursue your goals, regularly assess your progress and make adjustments as needed. Self-reflection, as discussed earlier, plays a critical role in this process. Use your reflections to evaluate what's working, what isn't, and where adjustments can enhance your progress. This ongoing evaluation keeps you aligned with your vision and responsive to the dynamic needs of your team.

Consider the inspirational leader's approach to pursuing her goals. She understood that the journey was as important as the destination and that setbacks were opportunities for learning and growth. By maintaining a flexible mindset and a commitment to continuous improvement, she consistently achieved her goals while also inspiring her team to reach their own.

Engage your team in the goal-setting process. Encourage them to set their own professional development goals that align with the team's objectives. This involvement not only fosters a sense of ownership and commitment but also reinforces a culture of growth and collaboration within the team. Support your team in their pursuits, providing the resources and guidance they need to succeed.

Remember to celebrate achievements, both your own and those of your team. Acknowledging accomplishments reinforces motivation and morale, encouraging continued effort and commitment to future goals. Celebrations don't have to be grand— sometimes a simple recognition in a team meeting or a personal note of appreciation can make all the difference.

As we move forward in this final chapter, we'll explore the theme of building a legacy of leadership. With the foundation of self-reflection and goal-setting firmly in place, you're well-equipped to consider the long-term impact of your leadership journey. Let's continue this exploration, ready to create a legacy that inspires and empowers future generations of leaders.

- Reflection and Setting Future Leadership Goals

As we reach the culmination of our journey together, it's time to focus on building a legacy of leadership—a lasting impact that extends beyond your immediate role and resonates throughout your team and organization. Your legacy is the culmination of your actions, decisions, and the values you impart to those you lead. It's about creating a culture that thrives on collaboration, innovation, and growth, ensuring that your influence endures and inspires future generations of leaders.

Consider the leaders whose legacies have influenced your own path. Perhaps they were individuals who embodied integrity, nurtured talent, and empowered their teams to achieve greatness. Their impact was not measured solely by personal achievements but by the positive change they inspired in others. In contrast, the Moron Manager's legacy was one of missed opportunities and unfulfilled potential, a cautionary tale of what happens when leadership lacks vision and empathy.

Your legacy begins with the culture you create. Foster an environment where values such as trust, respect, and collaboration are at the forefront. Encourage open communication and inclusivity, ensuring that every voice is heard and valued. This culture not only enhances team dynamics but also lays the foundation for a resilient and adaptable organization.

Empower your team to take ownership of their roles and support their development. Provide opportunities for growth and learning, and encourage them to pursue their passions and interests. This investment in their development not only enhances their skills but also reinforces their commitment to the team's success.

Mentorship is a key component of building a legacy. Share your knowledge and experiences, guiding others on their own leadership journeys. Encourage a culture of mentorship within your team, where knowledge is freely shared, and everyone is committed to helping each other grow and succeed. This collaborative approach ensures that your legacy is one of empowerment and collective achievement.

Consider the inspirational leader's legacy—her impact was felt not just in the results she achieved but in the leaders she cultivated along the way. Her commitment to mentorship and development created a ripple effect, fostering a culture of empowerment and innovation that endured long after her tenure.

As you build your legacy, remain open to learning and growth. The best leaders are those who continually seek new perspectives and embrace the journey of self-improvement. This commitment to growth not only enhances your leadership effectiveness but also reinforces the values of learning and adaptability within your team.

Reflect on the journey we've undertaken together in this book. We've explored the foundations of inspirational leadership, the art of crafting a supportive leadership style, the dynamics of change management, and the strategies for handling difficult conversations and conflict. We've delved into the transformation of meetings, the cultivation of future leaders through mentorship, and the navigation of common management pitfalls. Each step has been a building block in your leadership journey, equipping you with the tools and insights needed to lead with purpose and impact.

As you forge ahead on your business journey, remember that leadership is not a destination but a continuous path of growth and discovery. Embrace the challenges and opportunities that come your way, and remain committed to creating a positive, lasting impact on those you lead. Your leadership journey is uniquely yours, shaped by your values, experiences, and aspirations.

As we close this book, let's leave with a sense of optimism and determination. The world of business is ever-evolving, and the leaders who thrive are those who embrace change with an open heart and a visionary mindset. Keep your focus on the future, and let your legacy be one of inspiration, empowerment, and positive transformation.

Thank you for joining me on this journey through the art of effective management. May the insights and strategies we've explored together guide you as you continue to lead with confidence, empathy, and purpose. Here's to your success and the lasting legacy you will create.

www.ingramcontent.com/pod-product-compliance
Lightning Source LLC
Chambersburg PA
CBHW071051240526
45471CB00015B/1640